CULTURES OF THE WORLD®

LAOS

Stephen Mansfield & Magdalene Koh

Marshall Cavendish
Benchmark

New York

PICTURE CREDITS

Cover photo: © Michel Gounot/Godong/Corbis

AFP: 48, 51 • Axiom Photographic Agency: 11, 24, 35, 36, 61, 68, 73, 75, 76, 87, 90, 105, 126 • Crescent Press Agency: 20, 27, 59, 67, 77, 81 • David Simson: 3, 4, 14, 21, 23, 33, 34, 40, 41, 66, 69, 85, 91, 94, 103 (*top*), 106, 127 • Giles Massot: 26, 29, 32, 42, 45, 124, 130, 131 • Hutchison: 64, 70, 71, 79 • Lonely Planet Images: 1, 7, 43, 46, 114 • Photolibrary.com: 8, 49, 52, 53, 110 • Pietro Scozzari: 5, 6, 10, 16, 28, 30, 50, 60, 62, 72, 84, 92, 104, 108, 111, 120 • Stephen Mansfield: 9, 12, 13, 17, 18, 19, 22, 25, 31, 37, 38, 39, 54, 55, 56, 57, 58, 63, 65, 74, 80, 82, 83, 86, 88, 93, 95, 96, 97, 98, 99, 100, 101, 102, 103 (*bottom*), 107, 112, 113, 115, 116, 117, 119, 121, 122, 123, 125, 128

PRECEDING PAGE

Lao women in their brightly colored traditional outfits.

Publisher (U.S.): Michelle Bisson
Editors: Deborah Grahame, Mabelle Yeo, Mindy Pang
Copyreader: Sherry Chiger
Designers: Jailani Basari, Geoslyn Lim
Cover picture researcher: Connie Gardner
Picture researcher: Thomas Khoo

Marshall Cavendish Benchmark
99 White Plains Road
Tarrytown, NY 10591
Web site: www.marshallcavendish.us

Originated and designed by Times Media Private Limited
An imprint of Marshall Cavendish International (Asia) Private Limited
A member of Times Publishing Limited

All Internet sites were correct and accurate at the time of printing. All monetary figures in this publication are in U.S. dollars.

Library of Congress Cataloging-in-Publication Data
Mansfield, Stephen.
    Laos / by Stephen Mansfield & Magdalene Koh. — 2nd ed.
      p. cm. — (Cultures of the world)
    Summary: "Provides comprehensive information on the geography, history,
      wildlife, governmental structure, economy, cultural diversity, peoples,
      religion, and culture of Laos"—Provided by publisher.
    Includes bibliographical references and index.
      ISBN 978-0-7614-3035-3
    1. Laos—Juvenile literature. I. Koh, Magdalene. II. Title. III. Series.
DS555.3.M37 2009
959.4—dc22   2007048292

Printed in China
7 6 5 4 3 2 1

CONTENTS

Boys with their pet cockerel.

**Handicrafts for sale
at a souvenir shop in
Louangphrabang.**

INTRODUCTION

THE FATE OF LAOS resembles that of a pawn. First embattled, then conquered, and eventually abandoned, Laos has a history filled with much bloodshed and hardship. Ancient civilizations competed to subdue its kingdoms. Colonial masters raced to gain possession and bragging rights. Superpowers sparred to advance their ideologies for ultimate dominion. Caught in the crossfire, Laos still bears the scars of its civil wars. Decades after the hostilities, unexploded ordnance continues to claim innocent lives, and the country is still one of the least developed in the world.

Despite such adversity, Laos's rich heritage and wealth of natural resources have remained largely intact. Remote villages maintain their self-sufficient ways, ethnic groups still weave colorful costumes, and entire communities carry on celebrating both animist and Buddhist festivities. Life marches on according to the ebb and flow of the seasons, as the nation rebuilds itself socially, economically, and psychologically. The difference now is that Laos finally has the opportunity to chart its own destiny.

GEOGRAPHY

LAOS IS THE ONLY COUNTRY in Southeast Asia, a subcontinent consisting of more water than land, that is completely landlocked. It is the least populated country in the region. With a landmass of only 91,429 square miles (236,800 square km)—about the size of the United Kingdom—it is also one of the smallest. Laos's diverse frontiers, however, give the impression of a country that extends far and wide.

The country is bordered on the north by the Chinese province of Yunnan, on the northeast by Vietnam, on the northwest by Burma (Myanmar), on the west by Thailand, and to the south by Cambodia. Laos's landscape is dominated by the mountains of the north and east, as well as the great Mekong River and its tributaries. The high plateau of Xieng Khuang and the rolling Bolovens Plateau are the country's other main geographical features.

Laos is roughly 600 miles (966 km) long and 330 miles (531 km) across at its widest point, in the far northwest. In the narrowest part of the southern panhandle it is only 100 miles (161 km) wide, tightly walled in by the land bulges of Thailand and Cambodia. Military and colonial history has determined these borders, in the process denying Laos access to the sea.

Left: **Fishing boats in the Mekong River set amidst the lush forests.**

Opposite: **Limestone hills near the northern town of Vang Vieng.**

7

THE FLOODPLAINS

Laos has about 1.5 million acres (600,000 hectares) of rice fields. The floodplains also enable the Lao to grow wheat, corn, millet, sugarcane, sundry varieties of fruits, vegetables, rubber, and cotton.

About 70 percent of Laos is covered with rugged mountains and forested hills. Only the river plains and the shallow valleys can be cultivated for food production. However, such arable land is limited and consists of just 4 percent of Laos's total terrain.

During the rainy season the Mekong River carries great quantities of fertile silt, contributing to the region's agricultural wealth. The annual flooding of the river and its tributaries during the monsoon season ensures enough sustained moisture for wet-rice cultivation. The combination of tropical heat and rich topsoil deposits by the river has turned these floodplains into intensely fertile areas. Glutinous rice, which is the staple food of the Lao, is cultivated on these areas. Provided there are no disastrous crop failures, the floodplains can cater to the entire country's rice requirements.

The rivers are also an important source of fish. The generosity of these plains and the proximity of the life-giving Mekong explain why the majority of Lao live on or near the plains. Most of Laos's key cities are also located there.

The Lao have come to rely on the age-old seasonal patterns of flooding that have enriched their farms. In recent years, however, the thoughtless logging of forests located on mountain slopes, particularly in the north, has caused water levels to change. Adding to the flooding that has threatened the precious crops and livelihoods of the lowland Lao farmers is the construction of dams on the tributaries of the Mekong River as well as in the Yunnan Province.

THE PLATEAUS

The only other level land of any sort, apart from the floodplains, is on the mountain plateaus. The largest, the Xieng Khuang Plateau, is in the northern province of Xieng Khuang.

This vast area of rolling hills and grassland reaches an average altitude of about 4,250 feet (1,295 m). Phou Bia, which at 9,252 feet (2,820 m) is Laos's highest peak, rises at the plateau's southern edge. The soil here is poor, yielding few crops.

The central part of the plateau, an area of extensive grassland that supports an occasional tree, is better known as the Plain of Jars, or Thong Hai Hin. The name comes from the 300 or more stone vessels that remain scattered over the plain. The jars are roughly 2,000 years old, weigh between 4,000 and 6,000 pounds (1,814 and 2,722 kg), and measure between 1 and 8 feet (0.3 and 2.4 m) in height and 3 feet (0.9 m) in diameter.

The Khammoun Plateau is a beautiful area of limestone hills, rivers, jungle-smothered gorges, and underground grottoes located between the

The Plain of Jars. It is not known if the jars are rice stores, wine vats, or burial urns.

Laos has no railway system, and air transportation is still limited and costly. The Mekong remains the country's main highway, although steady improvements to its network of roads are now taking place.

The fertile lands in the Bolovens Plateau allow farmers to reap profitable harvests.

The Annamese Cordillera has always been a major barrier to transportation and communication as well as to invasion. Even now only a handful of passes cross the range.

Annamese Cordillera and the Mekong. The larger Bolovens Plateau lies in the southeast corner of the country's southern panhandle. A cooler altitude, plentiful rain, and fertile earth make the Bolovens Plateau, along with the lowland plains, one of the most productive agricultural areas in Laos. In addition to rice, fruits such as pineapples, durians, and peaches, all kinds of vegetables, and tobacco are cultivated on the plateau. During the French colonial period the area was well known for its rubber and coffee production. Decades of war and neglect have left much of this region in ruins, but in recent years coffee has become an important export for the country. The rubber plantations, however, continue to languish.

THE ANNAMESE CORDILLERA

A spur of the Himalayas that runs from Tibet to Vietnam, the Annamese Cordillera, or Annam Highlands, is Indochina's main north-south divide. The chain runs almost the entire length of Laos. The rugged northern mountains and hills form a series of steep, sharp parallel folds and ridges where rivers run through deep gorges. These mountains rise from 5,000 to almost 10,000 feet (1,524–3,048 m). The chain begins in the northwest of Laos and levels out in the southeast, dividing the watersheds of the region's eastern- and southern-flowing rivers.

THE MIGHTY MEKONG

The Mekong is one of the 12 great rivers of the world and the longest waterway in Southeast Asia. It flows for 2,800 miles (4,506 km) through six countries. From its source in the highlands of Tibet, it passes through China, Burma, Laos, Thailand, and Cambodia before flowing into Vietnam's Mekong Delta and out to the South China Sea.

Of all the Mekong countries, Laos occupies the longest stretch of the river. The Mekong and its tributaries run throughout the country and provide a much-needed source of fish, and its narrow floodplains enrich Laos's agriculture. Its waters carry tankers and barges, ferries, houseboats, pirogues, and sampans that provide transportation to people and freight along the length of the country.

Only a little more than half of the Lao section of the Mekong is navigable all year. Some of the northern stretches of the river—where there are rapids in the wet months and sharp, exposed rocks during the dry—can be navigated only for about six months of the year, and even then only by flat-bottomed boats.

The Mekong enters Lao life through a narrow, 125-mile (201-km) gorge that slices through rugged mountains along the country's border with Burma. The river widens a little farther east as it is joined by one of its largest tributaries. It then courses past Louangphrabang and Vientiane and onward to the southern cities of Savannakhet and Pakse. The river is navigable only as far as the Khone Falls, near the Cambodian border, where a massive natural barrier of rocks and rapids forms a series of thundering cascades.

NAM NGUM DAM

The Nam Ngum Dam was opened in 1971 with the help of funds and expertise supplied by the United Nations and the United States. The dam was built on the Nam Ngum River, a major tributary of the Mekong. The dam controls flooding along the Mekong and its tributaries. Its power plant generates electricity not just for domestic use but also for export to neighboring Thailand, thus supplying a good third of Laos's foreign earnings.

The Lao are very proud of the dam. Pictures of Nam Ngum Dam and its lake are featured on postcards and tourist brochures. The lake is dotted with dozens of small islands. Frogmen (scuba divers) using underwater chain saws have logged valuable trees that were overlooked before the valley was flooded.

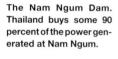

The Nam Ngum Dam. Thailand buys some 90 percent of the power generated at Nam Ngum.

CLIMATE

The temperatures are generally tropical to subtropical in Laos, depending on the altitude, the latitude, and the monsoon. The rainy season runs from May to October. The temperatures at this time are as high as 80°F (27°C) and above.

In mountainous regions such as Xieng Khuang, temperatures can drop to freezing in December and January. The hottest months are March and April, when temperatures soar into the high 90s on the Fahrenheit scale (high 30s°C). The coolest months are November to February, the first part of the dry season. The level of the Mekong drops dramatically at this time, revealing little islands and sandbanks that are submerged for the rest of the year. These are eagerly appropriated by the Lao and turned into attractive kitchen gardens for the cultivation of cucumbers, tomatoes, beans, pumpkins, and other vegetables and fruits.

Rainfall varies considerably throughout Laos. The mountainous northern province of Louangphrabang receives an average of about 50 inches (127 cm) of rain annually, while the Bolovens Plateau in the south averages 100 inches (254 cm). The wet months vary. In Vientiane, they are from May to September, whereas in Louangphrabang, August is far wetter than any other month.

Many cultural events are connected with the seasons and the climate. For example, the Rocket Festival, or Boun Bang Fay, in May sees the launching of giant homemade rockets that were believed to reach the heavens and bring back a deluge of rain. In addition, the end of the harvest season is a popular time for weddings and village festivals.

About 18 miles (29 km) south of Louangphrabang lie the Khouang-Sy waterfalls, a popular public spot.

Water buffaloes are a common sight in Laos. Like elephants, they can effectively work only in the mornings, when the temperature is cooler. They are mainly used to pull plows and carts.

FLORA AND FAUNA

Laos's forests are among its greatest assets. A varied species of tropical and subtropical trees cover almost half of the country. Deciduous trees and hardwood forests are found on the slopes of mountains and rain forest vegetation in jungle areas. In the north there are mixed forests with large stands of evergreens, oaks, and pines. In the cultivated lowlands of the south, mango and palm trees are common. On large plateaus such as the Plain of Jars, grassy savannas prevail.

Much of this green heritage is being threatened by illegal logging and commercial plantations. Many indigenous groups from the hills practice shifting cultivation, also known as swidden agriculture or slash-and-burn agriculture. Before any planting can begin, this harmful method of farming requires large tracks of land to be set on fire and then cleared with axes and hoes. The ashes add valuable nutrients for the crops. When the soil's nutrients are exhausted, the farmers move on to another piece of land, leaving the abandoned fields fallow for about 15 years.

Many animals, including some rare species, live in the mountains and jungles of Laos. These include tigers, leopards, rhinoceroses, lemurs, gibbons, several kinds of deer (including barking deer), wild pigs, crocodiles, cobras, kraits, and a wide variety of birdlife such as eagles, bulbuls, hornbills, pheasants, and hawks. Water buffaloes and elephants are trained to work. Elephants are used to haul large tree trunks from the forests down to rivers and roads. Traditionally elephants were used in the transportation of soldiers and supplies in wartime. The Khone Falls of the Mekong in southern Laos is home to the rare and endangered species of freshwater

A RARE CATFISH

Chicken sacrifices can be seen aboard fishing boats every April in an annual ritual offering to Chao Mae Paa Beuk, a female spirit who is believed to protect the *paa beuk* (PAH buk), a species of giant Mekong catfish. Measuring between 7 and 10 feet (2.1–3 m) in length and weighing as much as 670 pounds (304 kg), the *paa beuk* is the world's largest freshwater fish.

The richest fishing grounds for *paa beuk* are on the northern stretch of the Mekong near Ban Houayxay. These are fished in April and May, when the river level is low and the shoals of fishes are on their way to spawn in Lake Tali in China's Yunnan Province. This is when the ceremony of chicken sacrifice is held. The ritual takes place between Lao and Thai fishermen, who take turns to cast the large fishing nets required to catch these royal fish.

The flesh of the *paa beuk* is much prized by gourmets. But because the fish are in danger of becoming extinct, the number of fish taken from the river is limited to 50 or 60 a year.

dolphins. In the more remote areas of Laos, chickens, pigs, and even buffaloes are still offered in sacrifices to the gods, spirits, and ancestors of the village.

Every year several tons of endangered species are smuggled out of the country. This illegal trade of wildlife is ever growing and increasingly profitable.

THE CITIES

By Southeast Asian standards, Vientiane, with a population of just over 500,000, is a small capital. In 1563, King Setthathirat founded the capital, then known as Vieng Chan, to protect his kingdom against invasion. A former Buddhist center, the capital was raided and burned to the ground by the Siamese (Thai) in 1827 and was at the mercy of the jungle for several decades before the French took control of the country.

The government's new economic reforms aim to improve the city. For instance, the Friendship Bridge, completed in 1994, connects the Thai town of Nong Khai with Tha Nalaeng, a Lao river port, providing a further spur to economic change and development.

The three main urban centers apart from Vientiane are Savannakhet, Louangphrabang, and Pakse. Louangphrabang is the former royal capital and was named a World Heritage city by UNESCO in 1995. Savannakhet is near the Thai border and is an important trading post.

Laos may no longer be the Land of a Million Elephants, but elephants remain strong symbols in Laos. White elephants were once associated with royalty. They are still revered as symbols of good fortune and as protectors of the land.

HISTORY

THE GEOGRAPHICAL POSITION of Laos has always been central to its history. Surrounded by stronger and more ambitious nations, the country has been constrained by the Annamese Cordillera to the east and the Mekong River to the west. Its history can be described as a continuous struggle to keep its political unity and to maintain a strong national identity of its own.

Although the region of the Lower Mekong Basin is known to have been inhabited by primitive tribes as long as 10,000 years ago, there are no written accounts of the early history of Laos. Legends come before historical facts. For the ethnic minorities of Laos in particular, most of whom have no written records of their own, legends remain the only real way of explaining and passing down information about their origins.

Above: **Modern-day renditions of mythical figures said to be the first male and female ancestors of the Lao.**

Opposite: **The Patuxai in Vientiane commemorates the Lao who died in wars prior to the 1975 revolution.**

ANCIENT MYTHS

Legends about the origins of the Lao people take many forms. The best-known account narrates how the King of Heaven sent the first ancestor of the Lao, Khun Borom, to rule over the land. Seated on a white elephant, Khun Borom discovered a vine bearing two giant gourds. When these were pierced, men, women, animals, and seeds poured out. Using these resources to establish their own domains, Khun Borom's seven sons divided the land among themselves, thus founding seven Tai principalities.

A Khmer stone found near Vientiane suggests that the city may have been established in the fifth or sixth century.

EARLY MIGRATIONS

At this point historical facts and legends begin to merge. The Lao are a branch of the Tai people, who occupied a large area of Yunnan Province in China, long before recorded history.

The name *Lao* appears first in Chinese and Vietnamese annals during the shadowy period between the third and 14th centuries when the Tai peoples were migrating from Central Asia into southern China. By the eighth century, they had established the strong military kingdom of Nan Chao in Yunnan.

These Tai tribes continued moving toward the borders of present-day Laos, Vietnam, Thailand, and Burma. The pace of this slow, southward migration from Yunnan gathered momentum in the 13th century with the fall of Ta-li, the capital of Nan Chao, to the armies of Kublai Khan.

LAND OF A MILLION ELEPHANTS

The recorded history of Laos begins 100 years after the fall of Nan Chao with the birth of Fa Ngum in 1316. Fa Ngum, a Lao prince, grew up in exile at the court of Angkor in Cambodia. It was here that he studied and later adopted the Buddhist faith and married a Khmer princess.

With the help of the Cambodian king, Fa Ngum succeeded in uniting the Lao kingdom of Champasak in the south, Xieng Khuang in the northeast, the kingdom of MuAng Swa and its royal city, Louangphrabang, in the north, and the kingdom of Viang Chan, as Vientiane was then called. This brilliant warrior was also a champion of Buddhism, a creed that he made the state religion.

Under his rule, the borders of the country were extended to include large parts of southwest Yunnan, eastern Siam (Thailand), the Korat Plateau, and most of present-day Laos. Fa Ngum named the kingdom Lane Xang, the Land of a Million Elephants.

The work of Fa Ngum was continued by Samsenthai (1373–1416), his son, and the other rulers who followed. In 1563 King Setthathirat transferred the capital from Louangphrabang to Vieng Chan. A number of palaces, libraries, Buddhist temples, and monuments were built at this time.

After Setthathirat's death in 1571, Burma invaded the kingdom, which then fell into anarchy. After the arrival of King Souligna Vongsa (1637–94), a long period of peace and security followed, heralding Lane Xang's golden age. Ruling for 57 years, the longest reign of any Lao monarch, Souligna Vongsa further expanded his kingdom's territory and power.

At the height of its power, Lane Xang also achieved fame as a center of Buddhist learning, attracting monks and scholars from Siam, Burma, and Cambodia. It was at this time that the first Europeans visited the country.

An elephant mural at Wat Ipeng in Vientiane.

The That Luang temple was repeatedly damaged by invading Burmese and Siamese armies after the death of Souligna Vongsa. The French restored it in the early 20th century.

THE DECLINE OF LANE XANG

The decline of Lane Xang began with Souligna Vongsa's death. In the absence of a male heir to the throne, the country soon split into three separate kingdoms—Louangphrabang in the north, Vieng Chan in the center, and Champasak to the south. Each established its own alliances with powerful neighboring states. This stressed the divisions among the three kingdoms and prevented them from reuniting into a strong single kingdom. Between the 18th and late-19th centuries, these much-weakened states were riddled by invasions from Burma, Siam, and Annam (Vietnam) as well as by their own internal quarrels and instability.

Angered over foreign intervention and frustrated with the nation's decline, King Chao Anou of Vieng Chan suddenly rebelled against Siamese influence in 1826. The rebellion was short-lived; the Siamese armies captured and razed Vientiane, forcibly resettling thousands of inhabitants on the west bank of the Mekong.

With Vientiane now a vassal of Siam and gangs of Chinese marauders terrorizing the north and the east, the country was ready to fall prey to the hands of colonial powers.

FRENCH RULE

France's early interest in Laos centered on finding a river passage to southern China. French efforts to navigate the Mekong and open up a trade route halted when Khone Falls in the south proved impassable. The French then diverted their interest to exploiting the country's raw materials for their industries at home and in other colonies in Indochina.

By the end of the 19th century the French had succeeded in setting up a protectorate in Laos and had reunited its much-reduced borders into a single union. Although the French did little to develop the country and often neglected to involve the Lao in the decision-making process, their rule was, by and large, a mild one. It was under the French, however, that the seeds of an independence movement were sown.

The French saw Laos as a buffer state between its expanding empire and that of Britain. Laos helped extend French Indochina, while the 1893 treaty between France and Siam interrupted the advance of British India as well as British Burma and Siam. Under the new colonial masters the capital reverted to Vieng Chan, which the French dubbed Vientiane, and the country became known for the first time as Laos.

The tomb of French naturalist and explorer Henri Mouhot, near Louangphrabang. While exploring the tributaries of the Mekong River in 1858, Mouhot discovered the ruins of Angkor in Cambodia. He died of jungle fever in 1861.

Laos has the dubious honor of being the most heavily bombed country in the history of warfare. Unexploded ordnance has claimed and continues to claim many lives. At least 13,000 civilians—more than 40 percent of them children— have been killed or maimed by unexploded ordnance since 1973. The United Nations Development Program identifies unexploded ordnance as a key development challenge for Laos.

Bomb craters caused by American B-52s on bombing missions.

LAOS AND THE SUPERPOWERS

Laos was occupied by the Japanese during World War II. The inability of the French to defend Laos and the eventual surrender of the Japanese in 1945 gave great encouragement to the newly formed Lao Issara (Free Laos) movement. Although the French were to prevail for a few more years, full sovereignty was eventually granted to Laos in 1954.

National unity continued to elude the country, however, as it sunk into internal division and involvement in the political problems of its neighbors, particularly Vietnam. In the period known as the Cold War, Laos became the focus of global interest. The spread of Communism and the conflicting ideologies of rival superpowers—the Soviet Union, the United States, and China—soon transformed Indochina into a battlefield.

With different political factions vying for power, Laos soon disintegrated into civil war and a rapid succession of coups. The country was split three ways, among the neutralists, who officially represented the royalist

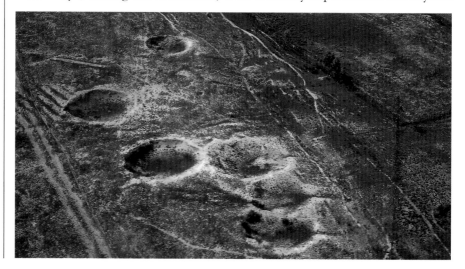

government and believed that a compromise with France was the best way to provide stability to Laos from Communist threats; the right-wing American sympathizers; and the Pathet Lao, a left-wing resistance movement strongly affiliated with the North Vietnamese Communists.

As the conflict in Vietnam escalated, Vientiane became a center for American undercover operations in the region. North Vietnam's main supply route, the Ho Chi Minh Trail, ran along Laos's eastern border. The Americans carpet bombed the trail, as well as the Pathet Lao stronghold, the Plain of Jars, and other strategic provinces. The United States also deployed a CIA-backed "secret army" in Laos, made up mostly of U.S.-trained Hmong and Thai mercenaries. By the time American troops began pulling out of Vietnam in 1972 and a ceasefire was signed in Paris the following year, more than 750,000 Lao had been forced to flee their homes because of the fighting.

The heroes of the Communist struggle in Laos are remembered today in the country's Revolutionary Museum.

Reconstructing their country has become a priority for Lao's present-day political leaders.

INDEPENDENCE AND BEYOND

With the decisive takeover of the country by the Pathet Lao forces in 1975, more than 600 years of monarchy came to an abrupt end. The king and his family, along with the royalist military officers and civil servants who had stayed on, were sent to so-called reeducation camps in the north of the country. With the abolition of the monarchy on December 2, 1975, the former Kingdom of Laos, the Land of a Million Elephants, became the Lao People's Democratic Republic.

The new government immediately faced a number of major social and economic problems. The end of aid from the United States coincided with an economic blockade by Thailand. Hundreds of thousands of displaced refugees had to be resettled.

To make matters worse, most of the country's qualified administrators, doctors, and engineers fled Laos. An exodus of businessmen, traders, mechanics, and artisans also ensued. In the 10 years following the revolution, more than 10 percent of the population, or 300,000 Lao, left the country as refugees.

Agricultural collectives were set up, religion socialized, and property belonging to members of the old regime confiscated. The economically unmanageable farming cooperatives were abolished in 1979 and replaced with moderate market socialism. The Soviet Union ended aid to Laos in the late 1980s, and in 1997 Laos joined the Association of Southeast Asian Nations (ASEAN), a regional grouping that promotes economic integration among member countries.

A steady improvement in relations with nonsocialist countries resulted in the resumption of international aid to Laos. Many Buddhist ceremonies and festivals associated with the country's traditional culture have been revived, and peace, stability, and even the prospect of moderate prosperity may finally have returned to Laos.

RECYCLING THE PAST

For the Lao who live in Xieng Khuang, even wars have their uses. Materials left over from the last Indochina war have been recycled into useful commodities. A brisk trade in recycled war scrap has grown over the years, with flare casings, bombshells, and pieces of airplane fuselages being collected and hoarded and then sold to scrapmetal merchants. These are melted down and resold for commercial use. War debris that is not sold is often stored by residents in the space under their stilted houses and then used when they can come up with a recycling plan for it. There are many examples of such resourceful use of war waste.

Many shell casings serve as fences, cattle troughs, water vessels, pillars to support houses and barns, and planters for growing vegetables. In one village a B-52 shell casing hangs from a frame at the side of the road, serving as a fire bell. Passersby may also notice bomb craters that have been improvised into harmless service as fish and duck ponds. Lotuses can often be seen blooming on the surface of these artificial ponds.

GOVERNMENT

SINCE THE REVOLUTION OF 1975, the official name of the country has been the Lao People's Democratic Republic (Sathalanalat Pasathipatai Pasason Lao). This is often shortened for purposes of business and correspondence to Lao PDR or, more simply, the LPDR. In French, it is the RDP.

The French designation, *Laos*, is still commonly used by foreigners and in most books and articles about the country. The Lao themselves refer to their own country as Pathet Lao. Pathet means "country" or "land." It is becoming common now among Western residents and diplomats to refer to the country as Lao, dropping the *s*, which the French introduced. The Lao people are sometimes called Laotians, but this too is being dropped in favor of "the Lao."

Laos is divided into 16 provinces, or khwaeng. *Each province, including Vientiane, which is an independent prefecture, is divided into districts called* muang. *These are further divided into two or more subdistricts or cantons known as* tasseng, *which are made up of villages called* baan.

Left: **The elephant and the national flag—symbols of today's modern Lao state.**

Opposite: **The parliament building in Vientiane.**

เลຂາທິການສູນກາງ ແລະ ກຳມະການສູນກາງພັກປະຊາຊົນປະຕິວັດລາວ

Posters like these show-ing the members of the political party are com-monly seen in govern-ment institutions.

The Lao government keeps a rare albino elephant to symbolically legitimize its power, as the white elephant also symbolizes the king.

ADMINISTERING THE COUNTRY

The central governing body is the Lao People's Revolutionary Party (LPRP). It is the only legal political party in Laos. The LPRP is directed by the party congress, which meets every four to five years to elect new party leaders.

The National Assembly (formerly the Supreme People's Assembly) is the nation's main legislative branch. Lao citizens elect members of the assembly for five-year terms. Numbering between 40 and 45 representatives, the assembly meets once a year to hear, discuss, and approve statements by the prime minister.

The executive government is nominally headed by the prime minister, who is appointed by the president of the republic with the approval of the National Assembly. The president is also in charge of appointing provincial governors and mayors. The National Assembly is responsible for electing and replacing the president of the republic. The current president, Lieutenant General Choummali Saignason, was elected in 2006.

Other important government organs are the Central Bureau of the Central Committee, a Permanent Secretariat, and the Council of Government, which consists of 14 ministries.

THE CONSTITUTION

Following the 1975 revolution, the government officially became Marxist-Leninist in its political philosophy. Communist rule existed without a written constitution for the first 15 years.

The first independent constitution of Laos was endorsed in mid-1991. Internal reforms took place, and several members of the old guard retired. At the same time, it was announced that the state motto, "Peace, Independence, Unity, and Socialism," would henceforth be "Peace, Independence, Democracy, Unity, and Prosperity."

A judicial system was set up, with the People's Supreme Court as its highest appeal.

The Presidential Palace in Vientiane.

French officials in Laos being escorted by a police officer.

FOREIGN RELATIONS

Relations between Laos and its neighbors have improved considerably in recent years. Violent border clashes with Thailand in the late 1980s have been resolved, though sporadic uprisings by Lao resistance groups based in Thailand continue to test ties. Visits by the Thai royal family and the opening of the Thai-Lao Friendship Bridge in 1994 have gone a long way to ensure that landlocked Laos has both an ally and an open door for trade along its long western frontier.

Relations with China have also thawed following a state visit to Beijing by then-President Kaysone Phomvihan in 1991. Laos is the only country in Indochina to have maintained relations with the United States since the revolution, even though the latter has never offered aid or financial reparation for the damage it caused to the country during the Vietnam War. Ties have strengthened since Laos agreed to cooperate over two key issues: the narcotics trade in the Lao section of the Golden Triangle and the search for the remains of American military personnel missing in action in the rugged Lao terrain. Relations improved further when Laos earned Normal Trade Relations status with the United States in 2004.

When Soviet aid ended, the withdrawal of most of its technical advisers and diplomatic staff made Laos turn more toward Thailand, the West, and Japan, its largest aid donor, for economic assistance. Trading partners Australia, France, and Germany also provide aid. Bilateral relations with Vietnam have remained cordial, but Laos's dependence on its old ally has weakened as it has developed relations with other countries in the region (such as its fellow Association of Southeast Asian Nations members) and farther afield. The withdrawal of some 50,000 Vietnamese troops from Laos in 1988 and the 1992 death of President Kaysone Phomvihan, who was half Vietnamese, further weakened the historical links between the two countries.

The Lao government hopes that in the future it will benefit from its role as a bridge between its powerful neighbors without being overwhelmed by them.

With the introduction of pro-capitalist economic reforms in the early 1990s, the old state emblem, the Russian hammer and sickle and the Vietnamese star, was quietly removed from all official documents and replaced by the silhouette of Pha That Luang, Vientiane's foremost Buddhist temple.

ຈົ່ງໃຊ້ຊະນາເຄດແກ່ເດັກນ້ອຍ

A billboard for the United Nations Children's Fund (UNICEF) in downtown Vientiane. UNICEF is one of several United Nations organizations active in the country.

ECONOMY

LAOS IS ONE OF THE poorest countries in the world. A huge foreign debt, a lack of skilled workers, and a per capita income of less than $500 a year paint a bleak picture. The quality of life, however, particularly at the social and cultural level, gives a more positive impression.

Most of the country's self-reliant villages produce sufficient amounts of food to live on and to exchange with neighboring villages. The system of agricultural collectives introduced by the communists proved unpopular and was soon abolished. Most farmers now own their own piece of land.

By 1979 it was clear that Marxist economic policies were not working. With the country tottering on the edge of bankruptcy, the government introduced sweeping reforms. The New Economic Mechanism, or Open Door Policy, was launched in 1986. By the mid-1990s capitalism had started to spread and take root, and its effects were beginning to show, especially in the cities.

The government began by loosening restrictions on private enterprise. State-owned businesses and factories that were not profitable were sold. Inflation has dropped from a runaway 80 percent in 1989 to less than 7 percent in 2006. The nation's gross domestic product has averaged a healthy 6 percent growth from 1988 to 2006. The Lao unit of currency, the kip, has remained stable.

In this progressive economic climate of ASEAN membership and trade resumption with the United States, foreign investors are looking more favorably at Laos. The flow of foreign aid into the country is welcome, as it helps balance Laos's loan deficits, at least for the time being.

Above: **Lao currency is known as the kip. In recent years the kip has maintained its value well, after years of instability.**

Opposite: **The modernization of Laos has fueled its economy, leading to a marked improvement in the infrastructure of many cities.**

AGRICULTURE

Almost 80 percent of the population is engaged in agriculture. Less than 10 percent of the country's total land area, however, is exploited for agricultural use. Glutinous rice is the staple food of the Lao. It is grown by lowland wet-rice farmers and dry-rice cultivators who are members of highland ethnic minority groups. Output has steadily increased in recent years, but a good crop heavily depends on weather conditions. Floods, droughts, a long cold spell, or a plague of rats can have devastating effects on the rural economy.

Other important lowland crops include corn, wheat, soybeans, fruits and vegetables, and cotton. Major cash crops produced in the mountain areas are coffee, tobacco, and cardamom. Another important activity in recent years has been livestock breeding, especially cattle and pigs.

Lao rivers provide a large and reliable yield of fish. Experiments in fish breeding have taken place in the massive reservoir that formed when the Nam Ngum Dam was built. If these projects are successful, Laos will be able to export freshwater fish to Thailand in the near future. Many rural people are dependent on the forests to supplement their diets and collect products such as cardamom and damar resin for sale. Increased hunting for food and extensive illegal trade in live animals and animal parts pose threats to the endangered species.

MINERALS

The remoteness of deposits had made mining uneconomical until now, but with improvements in the transportation network, more of Laos's mineral wealth is being explored. The country's rich mineral resources will prove to be a great asset in the future.

Planting rice seedlings is labor-intensive work. Laos produces more than 1 million tons (910,000 metric tonnes) of rice every year.

Laos has large deposits of lignite, iron ore, copper, lead, zinc, coal, and gypsum. Many of the areas with deposits have yet to be surveyed extensively. Other largely untapped resources include gemstones and gold. Australian mining company Oxiana is operating the Sepon gold mine. A number of foreign companies are surveying for oil, and many others have been granted mining and exploration rights. However, in the absence of concrete policies, high standards, and strict enforcement, the mining industry may cause harm to the environment. Rivers have been polluted, and rural life has been affected by resettlement, contamination of drinking water, and loss of livestock.

Laos's abundant forests include valuable woods such as rosewood, mahogany, ironwood, teak, and pine. Despite strict government-imposed quotas to conserve forest resources, illegal logging has been difficult to control.

FORESTRY

About one-fifth of Laos is still covered in primary forest. The plant life consists of teak and other valuable, high-quality hardwoods. More than half of the country's export earnings come from logging. Successive bans on excessive logging and a government reforestation program have failed to compensate for the destruction of Lao forests. More than 1,000 square miles (2,590 square km) of mountain forests disappear every year.

Corruption, lack of trained forest rangers, and porous borders make it relatively easy to smuggle wood out of the country. The activities of illegal loggers continue to reduce the country's canopy of green. Land clearing for hydroelectric projects worsens the problem.

Efforts by the government to limit the devastation caused by shifting cultivators, who destroy large tracts of forest each year for planting cash crops, have met with more success. Underskilled and undermanned, Laos has sought international assistance to implement its forestry program.

THE BATTERY OF SOUTHEAST ASIA

Along with timber, wood processing, and minerals, the export of hydroelectricity to Thailand is one of the country's greatest sources of foreign revenue. Most of this hydroelectricity comes from the Nam Ngum Dam north of Vientiane and the Xeset Dam in southern Laos. These account for more than $20 million a year in export earnings. The country's hydroelectric capacity is estimated to be almost 20,000 megawatts.

A power station at Nam Dong currently supplies the city of Louangphrabang with electricity. With the resurfacing of the northern stretch of Route 13, Louangphrabang will be linked to the Vientiane Valley power grid. Another project at Nam Theun, located on the Nakai Plateau in Khammoun Province, has plans to export 95 percent of the electricity generated to energy-deficit Thailand. When completed in 2009, this multinational collaboration is expected to earn Laos $80 million a year. More projects to exploit the rich potential of the river and its tributaries are likely to materialize in the future.

Even though Laos's hydroelectric potential is enormous, the rural population continues to rely mostly on fuelwood for its energy.

A market stall selling China-made toys.

INDUSTRY AND TRADE

Although the state has expanded the private sector in the hope of producing and manufacturing more goods for domestic use, Laos continues to depend heavily on imports. Foreign aid finances the majority of these imported goods.

The country's leading exports include electricity, timber, wood processing, tin, and the garment industry. Laos's manufacturing base, however, remains small.

Companies largely operate in the tobacco and food processing sectors. Sawmills, companies producing soft drinks, leather, paper, handicrafts, textiles, pottery, brick, and cement, and other small-scale enterprises are prominent too. Thanks to a steady flow of foreign investment into the country, more joint manufacturing ventures are probable. With a largely unskilled population of 6.5 million, however, Laos is unlikely to become an industrial giant in the future.

Laos's biggest trading partner, by far, is Thailand. Much trade is also carried on with France, Japan, and China. Imports, consisting mainly of oil and other petroleum products, machinery and motor vehicles, food products, and medicines, outweigh exports significantly.

FRIENDSHIP BRIDGE

Nothing symbolizes the economic awakening of the country better than the Friendship Bridge. The bridge, which was officially inaugurated on April 8, 1994, is the country's link to the world outside.

The bridge connects Tha Nalaeng, near Vientiane, with the Thai town of Nong Khai and is the first such construction to span the Mekong. The bridge, which is 0.7 miles (1.1 km) long, was financed with $30 million of Australian aid. The opening of the bridge was attended by a number of important people, including the Thai and Australian prime ministers, the Lao president, and King Bhumibol of Thailand. The bridge is a key link to the development of overland routes that will eventually connect Laos to Singapore in the south and Beijing in the north. The bridge has also been designed to accommodate a railway line if required. Rail links may possibly be built in Laos to connect northern Thailand and Yunnan Province in China with Hanoi in northern Vietnam. A second Laos-Thailand bridge across the Mekong opened in 2006, between Savannakhet and the Thai town of Mudahan. There are plans to construct a third bridge between the two countries, originating in Thakhek, Khammoun Province.

The Friendship Bridge. While happy with the bridge, Laos is concerned about the negative effects of unrestricted access to the country, such as crime, traffic, and environmental problems.

TRANSPORTATION

One of the major contributors to the country's economic development is the improvement and extension of its road network. There are more than 19,000 miles (30,578 km) of roads in Laos including national highways, provincial roads, local roads, and *routes coloniales* constructed by the French. Many are paved with asphalt, though the majority are unpaved gravel tracks. Route 13, running from Louangphrabang in the north to Vientiane, Savannakhet, Pakse, and the Cambodian border in the south, is the country's longest road. Other routes run east from this main artery and cross over the high mountain passes of the Annamese Cordillera into Vietnam.

Many road building and improvement projects are being financed by outside bodies such as the Asian Development Bank, the World Bank, and the Swedish government. This improved road system will help to transport people and goods more efficiently and safely.

TOURISM

Laos has become one of the most popular ecotourism destinations of recent years. In the 1960s few visitors traveled far beyond Vientiane and the old royal city of Louangphrabang. The war in Indochina led to a complete suspension of tourism. The country finally opened its doors to visitors in 1989 but with conditions. Since then tourist visits have increased by leaps and bounds. According to UNESCO, more than 1 million visitors entered Laos in 2005, and their numbers were expected to swell by 27 percent between 2006 and 2008. In recent years government support and collaboration with international organizations have improved urban infrastructures and tourist facilities a great deal. The government is worried, however, that allowing too many visitors will have an adverse impact on Laos's culture and way of life. Therefore it prefers to promote what it calls cultural tourism rather than mass tourism. Nonetheless, the country's rich history and culture, colonial buildings and Buddhist temples, magnificent natural scenery, and distinctive highland ethnic minorities are certain to attract more tourists in the future.

A bright hotel signboard welcomes potential guests. A relaxation of government restrictions on the movement of foreigners has helped increase tourist traffic.

ENVIRONMENT

LANDLOCKED LAOS BOASTS OF A wealth of natural resources. Its rugged terrain, limited industrial development, and low population density have nourished acres of flora and fauna. New plants and animals are being discovered. Some species that were once considered extinct have been sighted within its borders. Laos's National Protected Areas (NPAs) are important conservation sites. However, the fate of all its wildlife communities depends on how Laos resolves the conflict among development, resource exploitation, and environmental protection.

Deforestation, cross-border wildlife trade, dam construction, mining, commercial plantations, and urbanization threaten to sap the country's rich biodiversity. Environmental management in Laos has been hampered by a lack of equipment, funds, and skilled personnel. The remoteness of many areas complicates conservation efforts, while erratic law enforcement breeds illegal logging and encourages timber smuggling.

Left: **Elephants swimming in a river just below Tadlo waterfalls in the Bolovens Plateau.**

Opposite: **These rivers are at risk of pollution as Laos becomes increasingly urbanized.**

43

ENDANGERED SPECIES

Certain wildlife previously thought of as extinct has reappeared in Laos in the past few decades. Written about in 14th-century Chinese journals, the spindlehorn was sighted in the Annamese Cordillera in 1992. The rediscovery of the mammal, which looks like a large white-and-brown deer, along the Lao-Vietnamese border generated much excitement. Unfortunately the spindlehorn remains endangered, as its horns are a hunter's favored trophy.

The Indochinese warty pig is another creature that was previously thought to be lost to science. In 1892 a Jesuit priest purchased some of its skulls in southern Vietnam. The species was not seen again until it recently resurfaced in Nakai-Nam Theum, the largest NPA in Laos. The prehistoric Laotian rock rat, *kha-nyou*, believed to have been extinct 11 million years ago, was found among the lime rocks in Khammoun Province.

SHRINKING BIODIVERSITY

When Laos gained independence from France in the 1940s, its numerous forests were a wildlife haven for many plant and animal species. The International Union for Conservation of Nature and Natural Resources (IUCN) estimated that primary forests dominated half of the country's woodlands then. Today the figure has shrunk to a mere 17 percent. Because lush vegetation supports teeming wildlife, the animal population falls when the forest cover recedes and precious habitats are destroyed. In recent years there has been an upwardly spiraling demand for exotic cuisine (such as scaled anteaters, mouse deer, and squirrels), medicinal cures (such as bears' paws and snakes, birds, and insects bottled in alcohol), and accessories (animal teeth sold as necklaces, framed butterflies and beetles), further decimating their numbers. An increase in the use of firearms for poaching threatens the very survival of countless species of animals.

More than 400 bird varieties make Laos their home. In the 1990s British ornithologists recorded eight globally threatened and 21 near-threatened species, including the Asian gold weaver, the giant ibis, and the red-collared woodpecker. Unfortunately they are not the only ones dying out. Even the common sparrows are being threatened. The Buddhist practice of gaining merits by releasing caged birds into the open is being discouraged, as these birds often perish shortly after their release, being unable to survive in the wild.

DEFORESTATION

For centuries Laos's most valuable resource has been its forests. In 1940 they blanketed 70 percent of the country, but widespread deforestation reduced the woodlands to only 43 percent of the total land area by 2000. Despite passing laws on forestry management, land use, and resource protection, the government appears to have had little impact on logging and timber smuggling. Lao forests continue to vanish at an alarming rate.

Commercial logging is one of the biggest culprits. Timber is a major revenue earner for Laos. In 2005 significant amount of log

Deforestation is a common problem in Laos due to commercial logging and the increasing need for land.

was exported to various markets. Though there has been a drop from the all-time high of 25,920,965 cubic feet (734,000 cubic m) in 1999, organizations still continue to profit at the environment's expense. In return for building roads, the government allows Chinese businesses to take as much timber as they want from northern Laos. The national electricity company hacks ever-wider tracts along the highways each time it links a town or a village to the power grid. The army clears huge swathes of forests and benefits from timber sales to Vietnam.

Land clearing for agriculture, population growth, dam construction, mining, roads, and other developments have accelerated deforestation. The rapid loss of plant canopy results in soil erosion. Silt accumulates in rivers and irrigation channels, thus polluting water resources and threatening aquatic ecosystems.

PROTECTED AREAS

Laos's NPAs are recognized as among the best designed in the world. Many are in southern Laos, where natural forest cover is abundant.

In 1993 the government planted the seeds of conservation by establishing 18 National Biodiversity Conservation Areas spread over 9,498 square miles (24,600 square km), or 10 percent of the nation's landmass. Two more were added in 1995 for a total of 20 sites. Altogether they account for 14 percent of Laos and were renamed National Protected Areas. Only nine have functioning field offices to care for plant and animal life.

The most accessible NPAs are the Nam Ha NPA in Louang Namtha, the Nakai-Nam Theum NPA near the Vietnamese border, and the Phu Hin Bun

Laos has one officially declared national park, the Phou Khao Khwuay NPA near Vientiane.

A longboat crossing Nam Song, a protected area featuring limestone formations with honeycomb caves.

NPA, which includes the Khammoun limestone caves, east of Thakhek. The best time to view wildlife in these NPAs is in November, just after the monsoon season.

Unlike most other preservation areas, which forbid commercial activities, the Lao NPAs are divided into the following: production forests for timber, protection forests for hydropower watersheds, and conservation forests. There are plans to increase forest cover to 65,637 square miles (17 million ha), or 60 percent of total land area, by 2020. While the merits of a zoning strategy are clear, implementing such activities remains a challenge. The government's conservation commitments are also undercut by the logging and mining concessions it periodically issues within the NPAs.

You can do your part to protect the environment when visiting Laos. Dispose of rubbish properly, avoid restaurants serving endangered-wildlife fare, hike on established trails, patronize "green" tourism facilities, and report illegal practices to international environmental groups such as the Wildlife Conservation Society.

NAM HA ECOTOURISM PROJECT

Nature lovers and eco-warriors will rejoice in the Nam Ha NPA. Its 549,562 acres (222,400 ha) encompass 37 threatened mammal species including clouded leopards, black-cheeked gibbons, and wild elephants. Some 288 bird species, 18 of which are endangered, are also found here. More than 30 ethnic groups including the Lao Huay, the Akha, and the Khamu inhabit Nam Ha's undulating plains and towering highlands.

The UNESCO-sponsored Nam Ha Ecotourism Project is the longest-running community-based program in Laos. Launched in 1999, the project sees local partners working with the private sector to develop sustainable tourism, reduce energy consumption, educate people on the importance of ethnic diversity, increase environmental awareness, and promote responsible businesses.

For its contributions to poverty alleviation and heritage protection the Nam Ha project team won the United Nations Development Award (2001) and the British Airways Tourism for Tomorrow Award (2002). It was named an ASEAN Heritage Park in 2005.

The dam pictured above is located in Laos's Nakai Plateau. This Nam Theun dam is the country's largest hydropower project and was set to start operation in 2009.

DAM DESTRUCTION

The Mekong River sustains freshwater ecosystems as it travels the length of Laos. However, a flurry of dam construction activities are altering the natural environment and erasing traditional lifestyles in their wake. The government acknowledges the disruptive impact of damming but insists that the long-term economic advantages will outweigh the short-term negative effects.

Many experts warn that dams interfere with river flow, thereby destroying water quality. A changing water table of higher- or lower-than-normal fluctuations hinders the ability of certain fish to migrate and spawn upriver. Important fish breeding sites are submerged, and valuable ecologies are destroyed. Farmlands are flooded, wreaking havoc on the communities they support. Fishermen and villagers depending on fish as their main food staple are forced to relocate due to a decline of their numbers. Entire groups and their traditional way of life are lost.

Others argue that the cultural and environmental cost of damming is offset because hydropower is a clean and renewable energy source.

Unlike with fossil fuels, the process whereby hydroelectricity is derived does not pollute the air. Controlled irrigation enriches previously infertile soil and prepares new land for crop cultivation. Controlled flooding eliminates erratic flows and rapids, making it easier to navigate the Lao network of rivers.

Despite the controversy, government support for dam construction is strong. Lao officials believe that harnessing hydropower will reduce the nation's dependence on timber. The hydropower sector contributed 27 percent of export earnings in 2004, and further profits could help to cap commercial forestry at sustainable levels. Most important, hydropower could generate millions of dollars for a country where almost three-quarters of the population survives on the equivalent of less than two dollars a day.

Many visitors to Laos purchase saa—*paper crafted from mulberry tree bark. Compared with conventional wood pulp,* saa *needs little processing and is environmentally friendly.*

A common irrigation system found in farmlands.

URBANIZATION AND WASTE MANAGEMENT

Urbanization produces waste materials. Industrial effluents from textile manufacturers, sawmills, and food-processing factories are often discharged into open sewers and rivers. Refuse from small and unlicensed family-run businesses is disposed of randomly or burned. Almost all vendors operate with minimal environmental controls.

Currently the segregation of hazardous and nonhazardous waste is nonexistent. Besides providing proper facilities for garbage collection, the government needs to establish emission standards and regulatory controls on industrial pollution.

Sanitation services are hard to come by. Vientiane is the only city with a basic sewage system. In addition to the capital city, four secondary towns have modern disposal systems for solid waste. Other towns have to manage without such basic amenities, and even without safe drinking water.

About 1.5 million Lao reside in urban areas, but barely 55 percent of city dwellers have access to piped water. Rural areas fare even worse. To overcome these problems, the government is channeling more funds toward infrastructure development. According to a 2006 Asian Development Bank (ADB) report, 20 percent of all foreign aid to Laos will be used on improving urban water supply and sanitation.

ENVIRONMENTAL POLICIES AND TREATIES

Laos has passed a number of important laws governing the use of natural resources. The Forest Law was enacted in 1996 to ensure reforestation, sustained logging, and catchment protection. The Road Law in 1999 authorized environmental protection during road-building activities; companies that razed forests or destroyed property indiscriminately would be fined.

Laos has also ratified several international agreements. These include the Convention on Biological Diversity, the Framework Convention on Climate Change, and the Mekong River Commission Agreement. There is a high level of collaboration with neighboring countries in the Mekong region, as well as with international donors such as the ADB and the Swedish International Developmental Agency (SIDA).

Above: **An improvement in sanitation provides rural Lao families with access to clean water.**

Opposite: **Industrial pollution is a common problem for urban Laos.**

THE LAO

THE ESTIMATED POPULATION OF Laos in 2007 was 6.5 million people. In comparison with other Asian countries, Laos is sparsely inhabited, with a population density of about 73 inhabitants per square mile (28 per square km). The government is encouraging population growth. Improvements in health and sanitation have helped to reduce the high infant mortality rate, and children under the age of 15 now make up almost half of the population. At less than 56 years, however, average life expectancy remains low.

Above: **A Lao woman engaging in weaving work.**

Opposite: **A family belonging to the Iko tribe in Louang Namtha.**

More than two-thirds of the population live in the rural provinces, although a steady urbanization is taking place. The most populated provinces are Savannakhet (825,000), Vientiane municipality (700,000), and Champasak (600,000).

One of the country's greatest problems is the lack of an integrated population. Historically Southeast Asia has been a melting pot of races, cultures, and religions. Laos has the highest number of minorities in the region. The Lao Lum, the country's earliest settlers, make up 68 percent of the population.

There are four main ethnolinguistic groups. The Lao Lum are known for being the country's lowlanders; the Lao Tai dwell in the upland valleys; the Lao Theung occupy the mountain slopes and river valleys; and the Lao Soung, the country's highland dwellers, generally live at altitudes of more than 3,000 feet (914 m). There are more than 60 ethnic minorities in Laos.

THE LAO LUM

The Lao Lum are a subgroup of the Tai peoples who once occupied Yunnan Province in southern China. They learned about wet-rice farming and martial arts. This helped them to settle and gain mastery over the Mekong floodplains and to force other groups up into the higher areas. Today most city and town residents are Lao Lum.

The Lao Lum, who refer to themselves simply as Lao, are the country's dominant racial group. They are the architects of most of the nation's main traditions and institutions.

The official language of the country, Lao, is the dialect spoken by these lowland people. The Lao language belongs to the Tai sublanguage family, which falls under the Tai-Kadai language family. The state religion, Theravada Buddhism, is the faith of the Lao Lum.

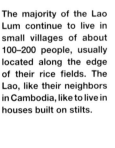

The majority of the Lao Lum continue to live in small villages of about 100–200 people, usually located along the edge of their rice fields. The Lao, like their neighbors in Cambodia, like to live in houses built on stilts.

THE LAO TAI

The Lao Tai, who mostly inhabit the mountain valleys of northern Laos, are closely related to the Lao Lum. They subsist as farmers growing wet rice, millet, corn, sweet potatoes, and beans as well as dry rice and wheat on mountain slopes.

Unlike the Lao Lum, the Lao Tai have generally maintained their animist beliefs and will go to great lengths to appease malevolent spirits. The Lao Tai distinguish themselves by the color of their clothing (Black Tai and Red Tai) or by the general areas they inhabit (the Forest Tai and the Northern Tai). The Lao government considers the Lao Tai to be part of the Lao Lum group.

Although Western clothes are becoming popular among the young, many Lao Lum women still wear embroidered, wrap-around skirts called *pha sin*. These are worn with silk or cotton blouses. The centerpiece of a Lao Lum woman's clothing is her finely decorated silver belt. On special occasions like weddings or festivals, a silk shawl called a *pah biang* is also worn.

A group of Khamu dancers and musicians.

THE LAO THEUNG

The Lao Theung are believed to be the original inhabitants of Laos. They are an Austro-Asiatic group who reside around the middle altitudes of mountain slopes. About 22 percent of the population belongs to the Lao Theung, the second-largest group in the country.

Their language belongs to the Mon-Khmer language family. Large numbers of Lao Theung are found in the north and the south of the country. Traditionally the Lao Theung lived a seminomadic existence as hunters and slash-and-burn farmers. Many have now settled on the land and cultivate crops such as rice, corn, cotton, tobacco, coffee, and tea. They usually trade with other groups by bartering supplies.

The Lao Theung often live with their extended families in large wooden longhouses built on piles. Made from bamboo, timber, and woven cane, the buildings are spacious and usually have high roofs. Some Lao Theung have adopted Buddhism. Others have remained animists.

Their place in Lao society has often been lower than that of other groups. They were known in former times as the Kha, or "slaves." Members of Lao Theung groups such as the Khamu, the Lamet, and the Lawa (also called the Htin) worked as court servants before the 1975 revolution. Even today, many Lao Theung work in poorly paid manual jobs for the wealthier lowland Lao.

THE LAO SOUNG

The Lao Soung, who represent less than 10 percent of the population, are the most recent arrivals in Laos. Their migration from China occurred only in the past 250 years. They are the most ethnically distinct of all the groups. Known in Laos as the Chinese group, the main subgroups are the Hmong, the Akha, the Yao, the Mien, the Ho, and the Lolo.

The language of the Lao Soung belongs to the Tibeto-Burman family. The Lao Soung are practicing animists. Elements of ancestor worship, Buddhism, and even Confucianism surface in their religious rituals, ceremonies, and feasts.

These highlanders consider themselves superior to the lowland Lao. This has often led to differences between the two groups. The Lao Soung are a fiercely independent people. Following the 1975 revolution many, especially the Hmong, fled abroad to escape persecution for fighting against the Communists. Many of those who remained in Laos were forcibly relocated from their mountain homes. Large numbers of Lao Soung are found in Burma, Vietnam, China, and Thailand.

Many of the Lao Soung are shifting cultivators, but they also live in settled communities. Villagers grow corn, cassava, mountain rice, tapioca, sugarcane, and root vegetables such as yams. They also breed animals, including water buffaloes and horses.

The Lao Soung are known for their excellent manual skills. Many of the groups produce tools, as well as silver ornaments and textiles.

A Hmong woman. Some 50,000 Hmong now live in the United States, having left Laos following the 1975 revolution.

HIGHLAND ETHNIC MINORITY FASHIONS

The apparel of the Lao highland ethnic minorities, particularly the clothes worn by women, helps to distinguish one ethnic group from another. In some cases, the name of a group can be guessed from its color and design preferences. For example, the main Hmong groups are described as Black, Blue, White, and Striped Hmong according to the color and type of their women's attire.

Styles vary greatly among the groups. The Hmong are known for embroidered designs, strips of colorful appliqué, and dyed pleated skirts. The Yao are noted for baggy trousers, long tunics, bright red ruffs, and the pom-poms that their children wear. The Lanten, a little-known minority, are distinguished by their white leggings and indigo trousers, as well as by the shaved eyebrows of their women. The Akha (*left*) are characterized by close-fitting headdresses decorated with coins, bright metal disks, shells, and beads.

Silver is regarded by the highland ethnic minorities as a source of wealth, almost like money in the bank. Silver pendants, chains, rings, bracelets, and breastplates are dazzling when worn against black, red, and indigo cloth. Some groups use old silver coins as earrings or necklaces or to decorate the borders of headdresses and skirt hems. Many are old French colonial coins; others come from China and Thailand. Old Burmese and Indian rupee coins from the days of the British Empire are found occasionally. Silver buttons beaten from coins are also considered important decorations.

It is not surprising that the strong visual appeal of the highland minorities' fashions have influenced Western designers.

The high ground occupied by the Hmong is also perfect for growing poppies, the raw material from which opium is made. This has been an embarrassment to the Lao government, which has largely succeeded in putting an end to the production of this cash crop by destroying fields and resettling the villagers.

OTHER COMMUNITIES

The Chinese are one of the largest foreign communities in Laos, as they are in most other countries in Southeast Asia. The majority of Chinese residents live in the cities of Vientiane and Savannakhet. They work as traders or run their own businesses. Many shops, hotels, and cinemas in Laos are owned by ethnic Chinese.

Another important minority are the Vietnamese. The French and later the North Vietnamese government encouraged their settlement. They engage in similar trades as the Chinese but tend to live in border and rural areas. There are a small number of Khmer (aboriginal Cambodians) living in the southern province of Champasak. They can be found in the trade and transportation industries.

With improved relations between Thailand and Laos, an increasing number of Thai are taking up temporary residence as businesspeople or education and aid workers. A small number of Indians, Pakistanis, and Bangladeshis have also made Vientiane their home. They are mostly shopkeepers, tailors, and tradesmen. Some of them can be seen selling fabrics and cloth every day at the large morning market.

These days a small but growing number of Europeans, Australians, Americans, and Japanese can be found living and working in Laos. Many of those who are not running businesses work for organizations such as the United Nations, the World Health Organization (WHO), or one of the many nongovernmental organizations such as the Red Cross.

A Vietnamese-Lao monk. Until recently, large numbers of Vietnamese lived in Laos. They still represent a significant minority.

LIFESTYLE

THE COMMUNIST REVOLUTION IN Laos tried to replace loyalty toward family, village, and pagoda with loyalty to the state. However, centuries of foreign incursions, the French colonial period, and the political doctrines of the 20th century have had relatively little impact on rural lifestyles and ways of thinking. Even today most people in rural Laos have little contact with the world beyond their village. Their lifestyles are largely prescribed by the seasonal routines of an agricultural way of life. Radical change and upheaval are contrary to the Lao character. As one Lao proverb puts it, "Let the dog bark, let the caravan pass by."

The Lao generally dislike extremes of behavior. Politeness, patience, moderation in speech, modesty, self-restraint, and respect for elders are important aspects of the Lao character that have influenced their way of life. The Buddhist idea that people should follow "the Middle Way" is reflected in the Lao distaste for conflict as well as in their willingness to compromise.

The ideals of modern socialist states, with their five-year plans and goals of national unity and construction, have left little impression on the largely self-sufficient Lao villages. For most lowland Lao, the predictability of the seasons and a generally reliable rice harvest have ensured a fairly comfortable and conservative existence in keeping with Buddhist teachings.

Capitalism, with the promise it offers of acquiring a new radio or motorbike, is likely to have a far greater impact on the life of the average Lao than any political theory ever could.

Above: **A young boy in his rural home sits on an empty shell while cattle graze in the background.**

Opposite: **Children enjoying rides in a park.**

THE RURAL CALENDAR

Annual patterns of work and life for most rural families are divided into two seasons—rainy and dry. The coming of the southwest monsoon rains in May signals the busy planting season. Most of the work is done by hand. There are few tractors or other agricultural machines. Oxen are still used to plow the fields.

Rice, once it has sprouted, is prepared in bundles and transplanted into corner sections of fields for a few days before it is planted in prepared paddies. During this time many villages hold ceremonies to propitiate the guardian spirit, or *phi* (PEE), of the rice fields. This period of intensive work lasts for about 100 days. The important task of weeding the paddies continues till the October harvest.

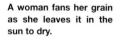

A woman fans her grain as she leaves it in the sun to dry.

During the growing season, men fish and hunt, repair things around the village, and make simple farming implements. The women concentrate on growing vegetables, cooking, and taking care of the house. With free time on hand they may do a little weaving. The care of livestock, such as feeding and bathing the buffaloes, is entrusted to children. This is also the period of Vassa, the Buddhist Lent. Monks retreat into their monasteries for the remainder of the rainy season. With the dry season, more intensive activity returns. There are ceremonies and celebrations to accompany the end of the harvesting, threshing, winnowing, and storing of the rice.

Except for the occasional bad year, crops are regular and consistent. This perhaps explains the general sense of satisfaction that prevails among most rural Lao. For the farmers of the dry mountainous regions such as those in northern Laos, circumstances are different. Variations in the weather and the poorer quality of soil hardly give them reason to feel secure.

Villages are usually built near a source of water. In the highlands, however, someone has to fetch water from the far-off rivers or valleys every day and carry it up to the mountain villages.

URBAN LIFE

Laos is the least urbanized country in Indochina. There are no cities to compare, in size or atmosphere, with the likes of Phnom Penh or Hanoi. The capital, Vientiane, is the only Lao settlement that remotely resembles a city, although Savannakhet is a developed commercial center, and Louangphrabang remains an important cultural hub.

Part of Vientiane's charm has always been its laidback personality. Its tree-lined avenues, crumbling old French villas, and riverside bars and cafés are reminders of a different age that remain untouched by the frantic rush of modern life. Recently some of that appeal has vanished with greater prosperity, the arrival of foreign investors and aid workers, and the influence of nearby Thailand. Discos, branded goods, Western clothes, and Thai television and pop music are now part of the Vientiane scene, for better or worse.

EDUCATION

Traditionally the education system in Laos was run by monks. Classes were held in the courtyard of the local pagoda. With the arrival of the French, secular schools were introduced and the French language taught. Some schools in Laos are still attached to monasteries, although the teachers are not limited to the monks.

The LPRP—the Lao People's Revolutionary Party—began a policy aimed at providing basic education for all children and eradicating illiteracy among the adult population. Although Laos's literacy levels remain low in comparison with those of neighboring countries such as Vietnam and Thailand, they are slowly improving.

War disrupted the education of much of the population. These young Lao, however, are making up for the lost opportunities of their elders.

More than a half-million Lao attend the country's primary schools.

Education is compulsory for all children between seven and 15 years old, but this is not always possible to enforce, especially in remote rural areas or among the seminomadic highland minorities. Primary education begins at age seven. Secondary education starts at age 11 and lasts for six years, but many students drop out before completion. A 2004 Human Development Report estimated that 38 percent of Lao students never completed grade five.

There are also more male than female students. Like others in Southeast Asia, many Lao families believe it is more important for sons to be educated than for daughters. About 77 percent of men can read and write compared with just 61 percent of women.

Founded in 1996, the National University of Laos is the only university in the country. Located in Vientiane, its nine colleges offer subjects ranging from forestry and agriculture to teaching and communications. During the 1970s and 1980s, many students were sent to the Soviet Union or Vietnam for higher education. This practice has stopped, but other things remain the same, including low pay for teachers and limited funds for textbooks and other educational materials.

HEALTH

Despite great strides in building up the economy in the past few years, the country's health standards and medical care remain woefully inadequate. This is reflected in its relatively high infant-mortality rate. About 81 out of every 1,000 Lao babies die due to malnutrition, diseases, and lack of access to proper medical facilities.

Public health care is concentrated in the cities, especially Vientiane, and is virtually nonexistent in remote areas. There is also a shortage of medical staff, with fewer than 600 doctors spread across the country.

The health structure was greatly damaged by the mass departure of many skilled doctors and other medical workers after the Pathet Lao's 1975 takeover, and it remains weak. Despite assistance from foreign organizations there is still a chronic lack of basic medicine, essential equipment, and experienced personnel.

In the countryside the widespread belief in the supernatural origins of illness has hindered some health programs, especially the immunization of children.

Drug addiction used to be a serious health problem. Laos had as many as 60,000 addicts in 1999, but the figure fell to 12,000 by 2006. Efforts to reduce the area of land under opium cultivation have been quite effective in lowering the number of addicts.

Women grinding grain. Females play a vital role in Laos's labor force.

WOMEN

The division of labor between the sexes in rural areas is almost as rigid now as it was generations ago. Men plow the fields, hunt, fish, build boats, fell trees, make basic tools, repair fences, and pursue other, similar tasks.

Women's work, if anything, is even more difficult. Women are responsible for running the household and bringing up children. In addition they are expected to cook, clean, spin and weave, carry wood, and tend the kitchen garden and are responsible for the backbreaking task of carrying and fetching water. They are also obliged to hull rice by pounding it in a large mortar with a heavy pestle. Women play an important part in economic activities outside the home as well. Most of the bartering and selling of produce in the markets are done by women.

Many women fought alongside men in the country's struggle for independence. Although women are now more highly educated than they were before the 1975 revolution, few real measures have been taken to improve the traditionally subordinate position of women in Lao society. In sharp contrast to Vietnam, where women have been encouraged to develop leadership skills, in Laos women have played a relatively minor role in its history. Politics remains an almost exclusive male domain, with very few women in senior positions in the government.

MARRIAGE

Arranged marriages are no longer common in Laos. Although the choice of a life partner is usually a personal matter, the heads of both families are consulted in advance of the wedding. The steps leading to marriage are complex. A formal request for the hand of the bride is usually made in the presence of a village elder or a monk.

Both families usually consult an astrologer to make sure that the couple's birthdays and fates are well matched. It is the parents who decide when the couple will marry, where they will live, and the sum to be paid as a bride price, or *kha dong* (kaa DONG). This is delivered to the bride's father on the wedding eve, when the groom's family will turn up at the bride's house with gifts of food, betel nuts, and other offerings.

Couples are married by village elders or a local monk in a simple Buddhist ceremony, which requires no exchange of rings. Traditional Lao dress is worn by both the bride and the groom; a *baci su khwan* (BAH-see su khwan), a distinctive Lao ceremony, is held, and sumptuous food is served at the reception. It is considered lucky to entertain strangers during the ceremony.

A typical family in Laos. For most Lao people, married life begins with a memorable ceremony.

Traditionally brides were abducted by the groom's friends and relatives in a pantomime of fighting and wrangling. In the southern provinces of Pakse and Champasak, the "kidnapping" of brides would take place with an elephant as the means of escape.

Many Lao women marry in their teens and start raising families early.

BIRTH AND ADULTHOOD

The naming ceremony of a newborn child is the first big event in a Lao's life. A *baci*, or ritual, in which money is attached to the infant's arms is held for family members, friends, and neighbors and sometimes for the entire population of a village. The size of the feast depends on the wealth of the family. A bonze, or Buddhist monk, is asked to choose a name for the child, one that will depend on the astrological specifications at the time of the child's birth.

For a boy, the next most important ceremony is one that marks his transition from childhood to adulthood. The manhood ceremony usually takes place around the age of 13. Only close relatives are invited to this ritual, which involves cutting off the boy's hair. In more traditional areas, boys still sometimes receive a tattoo as a symbol of manhood. This has the added value of warding off evil spirits.

DEATH

The final and most important ceremony for a Lao is the funeral. The ministrations of bonzes at funerals are mandatory and more marked than for birth or marriage. They are involved in almost every stage of the elaborate ceremonies up to the final cremation.

After the body has been prepared, it is placed in a coffin, and private family rituals are held. Expressions of grief are kept to a minimum. The Lao firmly believe that displays of sadness retard the rebirth of the spirit of the deceased into a better existence and block him from attaining the final goal of nirvana, or transcendence of suffering and desire.

After the family rites, the body is placed in a shelter in the garden or the yard, and a series of feasts and ceremonies begins. The body is finally taken to a cremation pyre on a riverbank or in a field. It is washed, exposed to the sky, and then cremated. Sometimes relatives burn jewelry with the deceased. The one who finds burnt gold while collecting the ashes is considered blessed, and it is said that the deceased wanted him or her to have it. The ashes are then kept in a small stupa at the village *wat* (what), or temple.

A funeral pyre about to be set alight.

Families who cannot afford these elaborate rituals resort to a simple burial in the forest. Graves are left unmarked in such cases, and it is hoped that all traces of the burial spot will vanish as quickly as possible; otherwise the spirit of the dead runs the risk of being influenced by malevolent spirits, which in remote areas are believed to harass villages and travelers.

RELIGION

THERAVADA BUDDHISM has influenced and shaped the Lao character more than any other single force. *Theravada* means "Doctrine of the Elders." Its followers claim that it is a purer branch of Buddhism than the broader Mahayana, or "Great Vehicle," school. Theravada Buddhists believe their sect adheres more strictly to the teachings of the Buddha, as set down in the Tripitaka ("Three Baskets" in Sanskrit), the Buddhist scriptures. Theravada Buddhism, sometimes known as the "Little Vehicle," is practiced in Sri Lanka, Thailand, Burma, Cambodia, Sipsongpanna in China's Yunnan Province, and Laos.

Theravada Buddhism has influenced the Lao in their conduct and attitudes. Little emphasis is placed, for example, on the accumulation of wealth for its own gain. It is a common practice for the Lao to set aside a part of their slender funds as a donation for the upkeep of the local pagoda or monastery.

Left: **Monks are respected figures in the community. Apart from their religious and moral duties, they are often consulted about family problems and matters of general welfare.**

Opposite: **Statue of Buddha in a Vientiane temple.**

Because it is forbidden to destroy any kind of Buddha image, broken images are piled up in temples, caves, and other holy places.

ADVENT OF BUDDHISM

Fragments of Buddha statues dating back to the Khmer occupation of Laos in the eighth century have been found in the Vientiane area. Buddhism was practiced in this region as early as the second century. It was not until the arrival of Fa Ngum and the founding of the kingdom of Lane Xang, though, that Buddhism took root as an organized system of belief in Laos.

Fa Ngum was known in Laos as the Great Protector of the Faith. It was Fa Ngum who carried the Phra Bang, a small golden statue of the Buddha, from the Khmer court in Cambodia. The figure was originally cast in Sri Lanka before being taken to Angkor. It is of immense importance to the Lao, who regard it as the symbol of Lao Buddhism.

King Setthathirat championed the Buddhist faith in the 16th century by building many temples and monasteries. During Lane Xang's golden age, Vientiane became an important Buddhist center in Southeast Asia. Its importance was lost after many temples were destroyed by the Thai when they ravaged the city at the beginning of the 19th century.

Buddhism declined even further after 1975 under the Communist regime. People were prohibited from giving alms to monks, and the teaching of Buddhism was banned from primary schools. These days, with increasing government tolerance and support, Buddhism is undergoing a revival. With many being restored and redecorated, temples are lively centers of learning and worship again.

BUDDHIST TEACHINGS

Lao Buddhists try to follow the example of the Buddha, born Siddhartha Gautama, the son of a Nepalese prince who lived more than 2,500 years ago in the north of India. Siddhartha's wanderings and meditations were rewarded when he attained enlightenment under a bodhi tree, after realizing the Four Noble Truths.

The first Truth states that life consists of pain, suffering, disease, old age, and death. The second emphasizes that these are caused by desire of and attachment to worldly things. The third Truth holds that detachment from such concerns can offer an end to suffering and the endless cycle of rebirth. The fourth Truth is that in order to free oneself from these, it is necessary to follow the Noble Eightfold Path.

The Eightfold Path consists of right understanding, thought, speech, action, livelihood, effort, mindfulness, and concentration. This is known as the Middle Way. It avoids two extremes—the pursuit of happiness

Devotees perform a Buddhist offering ritual.

through pleasure and through self-inflicted pain. The ultimate goal of all Buddhists is to free themselves from the tiresome cycle of existence and rebirth known as samsara so that they can enter nirvana. This ideal condition is often defined as "extinction of self" and can be described as a state of nothingness in which a Buddhist is finally free from suffering. In the Buddhist world view, the universe and all living forms are in a constant state of change from birth to death. After death comes the Wheel of Rebirth. There are three planes of existence in which beings can be reborn, depending on the thoughts, deeds, and speech of their previous life. These are the animal and ghost realms, the human plane, and the celestial one.

The Buddha's teachings are known as the dharma. It is the responsibility of Buddhist monks to pass on these teachings to the people. The Buddhist clergy, or *sangha* (sang-GHER), the Buddha himself, and the dharma are known as the Triple Gem.

All good Buddhists try to follow the commands of the Buddha as expressed in the Five Precepts—do not take life, do not steal, do not commit adultery, do not speak falsely, and do not consume intoxicating drinks. Any diversion from these Five Precepts in daily life postpones the achievement of nirvana. The accumulation of merit, however, makes nirvana more attainable.

ALMSGIVING

There are various ways in which Lao Buddhists can gain merit. Good deeds, acts of generosity, and respect for elders are common means to gain merit in the next life. The pagoda, or *wat*, is the center of village life. Merit can be earned by donating money to the local Buddhist order, helping with the cost of building a new temple, sponsoring a religious ceremony, or paying for the ordination of a monk. Most young men will undergo a period of ordination at some stage in their lives. This is one effective way for a son to acquire merit for his family, especially because his mother and sisters, being women, cannot be ordained.

Monks depend upon the local population for most of their material needs. Pagodas are always located near population centers. Everyone has an opportunity to earn merit each morning by offering alms to monks as they walk through the streets at dawn asking for alms. In Laos it is mainly women who can be seen earning merit in this way. The women place rice, vegetables, and other delicacies into the monks' bowls as they pass.

Monks on an alms round. The monk gives no thanks for the offerings he receives. Because gifts of this kind are a chance to acquire merit, gratitude is not expressed or expected. It is the giver, in fact, who thanks the monk for providing the chance to feed him and gain merit by the act.

Traditionally Lao males spend three months in the monastic order during Buddhist Lent, but nowadays some spend only a week to 15 days acquiring merit.

77

IMAGES AND MUDRAS

Buddha images, especially statues, have survived war and destruction better than Lao temples. Unlike old bomb casings, bronze and gold Buddhas are never melted down, however ruinous their condition. Buddha images throng the insides of temples, monasteries, and sacred caves. They can be seen standing in the open along the roadside, commanding the crest of a hill, or ranged along the external pavilions of temples.

Apart from being works of art, they are also objects of worship. Images are represented in different mudras, or attitudes. Ancient Pali texts and Sanskrit poetry have set down certain characteristics of the Buddha that have influenced Lao artists.

The Buddha is usually represented sitting, standing, lying, or less commonly, walking. There are about 40 mudras. Lao Buddhas have some unique features. These include elongated ears, a sharp beaked nose, and surprisingly slender waists. The following are some of the most popular mudras used in depicting the Buddha in Laos:

THE BUDDHA CALLING FOR RAIN In this mudra, the Buddha is standing with his hands pointing down toward the earth. This image is rarely found outside of Laos.

***BHUMISPARCAMUDRA* (boo-miss-PAH-cam-moo-DRAH)** Also referred to as "Touching the Earth" or "Calling the Earth Goddess to Witness," this mudra depicts the Buddha's enlightenment and victory over Mara, king of the demons. The Buddha's right hand is placed over his right knee. His fingers point to the earth.

A typical Lao mudra. The figure's right hand is reaching across his knee to touch the earth.

DHYANAMUDRA (yan-AH-moo-DRAH) This is a common image in which the Buddha is seen meditating. His open palms face upward, resting on his lap.

ABHAYAMUDRA (ab-hay-YAH-moo-DRAH) This means "Giving Protection" or "Dispelling Fear." The Buddha's right palm is usually raised in front of his chest as if holding back evil.

A sacred cave at Vang Vieng. Many Lao villages have a spirit grove where the *phi* live.

SPIRIT GROVES

If Buddhism is the primary religion of the lowland Lao, then animism (spirit worship) is the dominant belief of many highland ethnic minorities, who believe that spiritual beings inhabit certain forest groves. For most Lao, there is no contradiction in observing both Theravada Buddhism and animist practices. The Lao Lum's belief in *phi,* or spirits, plus the attendant superstitions and rituals coexist happily with Buddhism.

The belief in *phi* is often combined with ancestor worship. There are basically two types of spirits that the Lao pay attention to—mischievous or malignant ones and guardian spirits. Evil spirits may be spirits of the dead or spirits of a place. Lao villagers and mountain dwellers are careful to avoid jungles and lonely, unexplored places at night. One widespread belief is that it is dangerous to walk on all fours in the forest. Anyone who does this runs the risk of being possessed by a tiger spirit. It is also inadvisable to walk along a lonely riverbank at night in case a water spirit attacks. This would cause the person to believe he is a fish, and lengthy and costly offerings would have to be made to the spirit before the person could be released.

The Lao spend as much time making offerings to ensure the favor of the guardian spirits as they do to appease the evil ones. Rituals to Nang Prakosob, the female spirit of rice, for example, must be carefully observed to ensure a good harvest. Most villages have two main protective spirits—the *phi wat,* guardian of the temple, and the *phi muang*, protector of the village. In Vientiane the Chao Mae Si Muang is believed to be the guardian of the city. Local Lao go to Wat Si Muang to ask for her favor and make offerings.

OTHER RELIGIONS

Laos's 1991 constitution guarantees freedom of religious belief. The majority of Lao, however, feel comfortable and content with their unique mixture of Buddhism and animism and show little interest in converting to other faiths.

In the aftermath of the 1975 revolution, Christian missionaries were expelled from the country. The current Lao constitution forbids religious proselytizing, or actively seeking to convert others to a particular religion. Foreigners caught distributing religious materials risk being arrested and deported.

Most Christians are found among either the French-educated Lao class that remained in the country after 1975 or animist highland ethnic minorities who were converted by Christian missionaries and priests operating under the umbrella of various nongovernmental organizations in the country's remote areas.

Islam has had little impact on Lao life. There is a very small number of Muslims living in Vientiane. Most Lao Muslims are of Pakistani or Arab extraction. Many of them have married Lao women, who as

A French cathedral. There are four Apostolic Vicariates in Laos.

spouses are given the constitutional right to convert to Islam. Others are descendants of the Cham Muslims from Cambodia, who fled Pol Pot's brutal persecution in the 1970s. A few groups of Muslim Yunnanese also live in northern Laos.

81

THE *JATAKA* TALES

Printing was only introduced to Laos in 1957. Before that, Lao literature was written in the manuscript form. Many manuscripts were engraved on palm leaves. Some of these have survived and are kept in museums or in the libraries of monasteries and temples. Some of the most interesting manuscripts are those that contain the *jataka* (jah-TAK-er) tales.

The *jataka* tales are central to Buddhist literature. This collection of stories concerns the previous *jataka*, incarnations or lives, of the Buddha. These former existences of the Buddha are called Bodhisattvas. The tales describe the long journey of the Buddha and his passage through the various animal states and human conditions to his final attainment of nirvana. The stories are a colorful vehicle for Hindu folklore and fables, the teaching of Buddhist ethics, satirical asides, and even humor. Fifty Lao *jataka* recounting local folktales have been added to the original 547 tales that appear in Pali. The most popular *jataka* in Laos is the story of Prince Vessantara's perfect renunciation of the world, which is also known as *Phra Vet* in Lao.

The stories are painted in bright, often garish colors on the outside walls of temples and shrines. They are often painted in panels that resemble a comic strip. The Lao enjoy the stories just as much for their entertainment value as for their religious and moral aspects.

THE PAK OU CAVES

The impressive Pak Ou Caves are located opposite the mouth of the Nam Ou, a tributary of the Mekong, some 15 miles (24 km) north of Louangphrabang. They are set dramatically into limestone cliffs overhanging the Mekong River. The upper cave is known as Tham Phun, the lower as Tham Thing. The two main caves are sanctuaries for thousands of Buddha images.

The caves were discovered by King Setthathirat in the 16th century. The statues, made of wood and gold, are more than 300 years old. Many of them were brought here for safekeeping during periodic attacks on Louangphrabang. The statues vary in height from just a few inches to 6 feet (1.8 m). Many of the statues have been carved in classic attitudes such as the Buddha Calling for Rain.

Once inhabited by monks, the caves are now believed to be the home of guardian spirits. The Pak Ou Caves are sacred to the Lao, and a visit here is seen as a pilgrimage. Before the revolution the Lao king used to visit the caves every year during the Pi Mai (Lao New Year) festival and conduct a candle-lighting ceremony. Hundreds of people still make the trip in boats from Louangphrabang during the festival to make offerings and light candles in the gloom of these sanctuaries.

More than half of the population of Laos are practicing Buddhists. Many of the highland ethnic minorities maintain a primitive belief in spirit worship and supernatural forces. Even the Buddhism practiced by people in the cities retains a uniquely Lao character, incorporating centuries-old elements of animism, Brahmanism, and ancestor worship.

ຕ ສ້ວມາ ຈຳພຸດ ຫ຾

ຫັດຫົງວາຍຍຍະ ຫຶດ

ໄດ້ສ້າເຈຕິຍັງຊຸຮ້າຖ

ໃຫະ ວະຮ້າຊຊະຕຳສາ

ະ ຫາກກາດ ສະ ເຂ ສະ ກາ

ກ ຊຮະ ຫັງເຕຫັງ ຮາຍ

ຮະ ສ້າວງຫ້າຍໂ ເຕຈະ ຫ

ຶ ສ ຫາຍົ ສ່ຍພະ ຫາ

LANGUAGE

LAO, THE OFFICIAL LANGUAGE of the LPDR, belongs to the Tai group of languages under the Tai-Kadai linguistic family. Tai is part of a language family that extends from Assam in India to Yunnan Province in southern China. There are Tai speakers in northern parts of Vietnam, Burma, Thailand, and pockets of China such as Guangxi and Sichuan. Together the number of Tai speakers is close to 900 million.

Standard Lao as spoken in the region around Vientiane has become the lingua franca of most Lao, including ethnic minorities who may have their own distinct languages and dialects. The Lao spoken today is quite different from the language spoken before the revolution. Many honorifics and other respectful forms of address disappeared as the regime tried to create a classless society. Large population movements after the war have introduced into the language local and regional words that have become part of a common, shared vocabulary.

Left: **A Lao television reporter and camera crew at work. A domestic television service started in December 1983.**

Opposite: **Lao script engraved on stone.**

THE TONAL SYSTEM

Lao is a monosyllabic, tonal language. Most of the polysyllabic words found in Lao are borrowed from two ancient Indian languages, Pali and Sanskrit. Words have also crept in from Khmer, French, English, and even Persian. Spoken Lao uses six tones: three level tones (high, midrange, and low), one rising tone, and two falling ones. As with most other languages, the pitch at which the language is spoken is not absolute and will vary from speaker to speaker.

There are 33 consonants in Lao—27 are single consonants and 6 are double—which can be classified into three groups: low, high, and rising. Because almost all the high and rising consonants have identical sounds, the 33 consonants produce only 20 distinct sounds in all. There are 28 vowel sounds in Lao. These are divided into long and short sounds.

An example of the Lao script. Before 1975 there were very few printing presses in Laos. Textbooks and advanced manuals were printed in either Thai, French or Vietnamese.

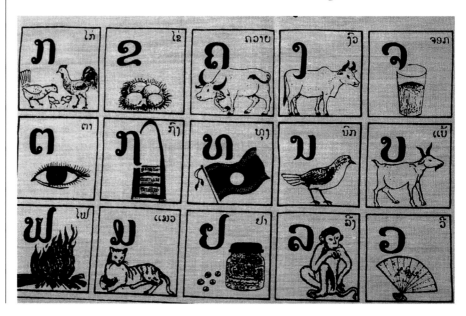

A slight change in inflection can drastically alter the meaning of a word. The word *khaa* (car), for example, can mean "crow" in a low level tone, "price" in the midtone, and "to kill" in a low, falling tone.

Although Lao grammar is surprisingly straightforward the tonal system can, at least initially, be a stumbling block for foreigners wishing to learn the language.

THE LAO SCRIPT

Like Cambodian, Thai, and Burmese, written Lao has its origins in the ancient scripts of southern India. The oldest written documents still in existence in Laos date back to the 16th century.

Lao manuscripts, or *kampi* (kem-PI), were usually engraved on palm leaves and then threaded together with cord. Sets of 20 leaves were bundled together and wrapped in cloth for safekeeping, but many have suffered from the passage of time, the tropical climate, and insect attacks.

Other scripts have been used throughout the centuries in Laos. These include scripts for spoken Yao and for written Pali, a Thai Neua tribal script, and a Chinese-based system used in the 16th century. Modern Lao is written from left to right. There are no spaces between words.

A trishaw passes by a building signboard.

There were four spelling systems in use before the revolution. These have been standardized into one single phonetic script that expresses both the sound of the word and its pitch.

LAO AND THAI

The Lao and the Thai understand each other very well. Standard Thai is similar enough to Lao for the two to be mutually intelligible, much like the relationship between spoken Portuguese and Spanish. Most of the present-day differences stem from the French colonial period, when Lao was insulated from ongoing changes in the Thai language.

A Thai dialect spoken in the north of Thailand, particularly its northeastern province of Esan—which was originally part of the Lao kingdom of Lane Xang—is virtually the same as Lao. Strangely, there are supposedly more Lao speakers living in this region of Thailand than there are in Laos itself.

Because most of the textbooks used at the university level were and continue to some extent to be in Thai, many educated Lao can understand the written script as well. Thanks to the popularity of Thai television and radio programs that are transmitted daily over the Mekong, almost all Lao can understand spoken Thai.

LANGUAGES OF THE MINORITIES

Russian linguists in the 1980s estimated that the highland ethnic minorities of Laos had more than 600 spoken dialects. Numerous local dialects, branches, and subdivisions of Tai languages are mutually intelligible to the respective groups. With the exception of one or two groups such as the Yao, very few of the tribal groups have their own written script. Important language families that exist among the highland ethnic minorities of Laos include:

TIBETO-BURMESE The Lahu, the Lisu, and the Akha are examples of tribes that speak dialects within this group. They are mostly concentrated in the northern region of Laos.

HMONG-YAO This important group originated in southern China and includes the Mun language of the Lanten. Groups of Hmong are found in China, Thailand, and northern Vietnam.

MON-KHMER More than 30 tribal groups speak dialects that fall into this language family. The best known are the Alak, the Soh, and the Suei, who live in the south; the Lamet, from the north; and the Pai and the Khamu, who can be found all over Laos.

New propaganda murals are often produced and old ones touched up before special events such as Lao National Day, a public holiday that celebrates the 1975 revolution with street parades and speeches.

FRENCH AND ENGLISH

Up until the early 1990s, French was the preferred second language of the educated Lao class, government workers, and administrators. Even now it remains the country's official second language. Shop signs, restaurant menus, and some legal documents are often still written in French with Lao translations. The language is falling out of favor among the younger generation, however.

Like their neighbors in Vietnam and Cambodia, young Lao prefer to learn English instead of French. They believe that a basic knowledge of English will enhance their career prospects, especially in the fledgling tourism sector, and help them acquire high-paying jobs.

PROVERBIALLY YOURS

Lao, in common with other languages, contains a rich and colorful assortment of proverbs. Many reflect aspects of the national character and ways of thinking, the nation's culture, the folklore of the highland ethnic minorities, and even the geographical features of the country. The following is a small selection from the hundreds that exist in the Lao language:

When one has heard, one must listen, and when one has seen, one must judge with one's heart.

Medicine can cure the bite of a poisonous snake, but nothing can master a wicked heart.

When the buffaloes fight it is the grass that suffers.

A tray full of money is not worth a mind full of knowledge.

Some are brave in the village but cowards in the forest.

When the water level falls, the ants eat the fish. When the level rises, the fish eat the ants.

An empty pot makes a loud noise.

Do not soil the shade of a tree that has been hospitable to you.

Opposite: **"Learning English is ABCD,"** proclaims this schoolboy's bag. Like much of the rest of the world, the Lao are beginning to realize the economic importance of English.

ARTS

FOR CENTURIES LAOS HAS been the target of foreign domination and greed. Its towns and cities have been plundered and its treasures removed. Given that Laos was repeatedly ransacked by the Thai, the Chinese, and the Vietnamese and then bombed by the Americans, it is surprising that so much of its cultural heritage has survived.

Although Lao culture has its roots in many nearby countries, it is distinct from that of its Southeast Asian neighbors. The country has its own architecture, music, written language, handicrafts, dress, and popular customs. Decades of war, civil strife, and revolution, however, have left their mark on this fragile nation. Now that peace, security, and the prospect of modest prosperity have come to the historically contentious countries of the Mekong, a modest revival of the arts is beginning to take place in Laos.

Left: **Gold-painted wooden panels at Wat Xieng Thong. The Lao have excelled at wood carving for centuries.**

Opposite: **Traditional Lao cloths with their signature bright colors.**

LITERATURE

Lao literature, like that of neighboring Thailand and Cambodia, presents a strong imprint of Indian influence. Laos has a strong oral tradition—folk stories were recited, while epic poems and verse novels were usually sung or chanted by professional storytellers and balladeers. The most famous work in Lao literature, an epic poem called *Sin Xay,* was originally sung.

The arrival of Buddhism in the 14th century introduced more Lao to the written language. People began recording the stories they had heard. Classical tales focus on love, heroic deeds, mythology, and the history of the gods. Religious literature, such as the *jataka* tales, deals with the Buddha's birth and various forms of existence. One popular story involves

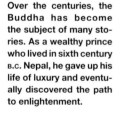

Over the centuries, the Buddha has become the subject of many stories. As a wealthy prince who lived in sixth century B.C. Nepal, he gave up his life of luxury and eventually discovered the path to enlightenment.

a legend about the Buddha footprint found on Mount Phousi in Louangphrabang. Unfortunately many Lao manuscripts were taken to Bangkok after the Thai razed the capital in 1828.

Historical chronicles were traditionally written in Pali by anonymous authors. The best known is *Nithan Khun Borom* (*The History of King Khun Borom*). Many Lao popular stories and novels are based on the Indian canon of tales called *Panchatantra*, where adventurous and supernatural themes dominate. Tales about animals who have human characteristics are also popular. Some are reminiscent of Aesop's fables. These are contained in several volumes of stories titled *The Bull*, *The Frogs*, *The Demons*, and *The Birds*. Echoes of another familiar story, *Cinderella*, can be found in the Lao tale *Pa Pul Dan*, about a young girl and her selfish stepmother.

Laos has a short history of written literature. Printing was introduced during French colonial rule, and the country's first modern novel, *The Sacred Buddha Image*, was published in 1944. Decades of civil war followed by Communist rule have hampered literary development, as the population has been more concerned with day-to-day living than with the arts. Popular author Ounthine Bounyavong's *Mother's Beloved: Stories from Laos* was published in 1999. It was the first instance of contemporary Lao fiction.

A close-up of a carved manuscript box previously used to store numerous literary gems.

THE LAO RAMAYANA

The Ramayana, or Ramakien, is an epic verse play written by the Indian poet Valmiki. The Hindu drama, which tells the story of the Indian king Rama and his wife, Sita, is performed all over Southeast Asia. Its influence on the region's arts and culture has been enormous.

The Lao version of the Ramayana is known as *Pra Lak Pra Lam*. Although it follows the original story by outlining the life of Rama and Sita, the Lao version has many original features. The action takes place not in India but along the Mekong Valley. The first 20 pages of the Lao version describe the geography and landscape of Laos.

Subplots, local myths, and folklore have been added to the original. Although the story remains basically the same, the background scenery has been changed and characters adapted in such a way that any Lao would recognize and adopt the setting and morality of the story as his own.

Dancers rehearse some of the finger movements needed to perform the Lao version of the Ramayana. Scenes from the Ramayana can be seen all over Laos. Dance dramas enact scenes such as the monkey god, Hanuman's, battles and the abduction of Sita. Figures and scenes from the Ramayana are also found in the many murals and carvings of Lao temples.

NAGA *SYMBOLISM*

Lao art and legends are full of stories and images of *naga* (NAR-ger). The *naga*, or *nak* (nak), as it is better known in Laos, is a mythical water serpent that resembles a cobra. It was an important symbol in Southeast Asia even before the advent of Buddhism or Hinduism in the region.

The *naga* is a symbol of both destruction and renewal. In Hindu-Buddhist legends, a *naga* was responsible for causing a great drought to spread over the earth after it drank all the water. An ancient Khmer legend relates how a king, whose domains were suffering from a terrible drought, fired rockets into the sky; the god Shiva was so pleased that he let the rains fall. Many of the rockets used in the May Rocket Festival are decorated to resemble *nagas*.

Buddha is believed to have been protected by the hood of a *naga* when facing the demon Mara. *Naga* images appear all over Laos. Their mouths are always open, and their heads may look like those of snakes or dragons. *Naga* heads frequently support the roofs of temples. Temple entrances are often guarded by five- or seven-headed *nagas*. Single *nagas*, their bodies stretched to fantastic lengths, may decorate the balustrades of staircases leading up to hilltop temples. They are placed there to symbolize a bridge between two worlds—the earthly and the spiritual. They provide a good example of the way ancient myths, legends, and folk symbolism in Laos are interwoven with orthodox Buddhism.

The prow of a racing boat designed in the form of a *naga* head.

WAT XIENG THONG

Wat Xieng Thong is the most important royal temple in Louangphrabang. Built in 1559 by King Setthathirat, it is the only building of its kind to have survived the succession of raids that plagued the city in the 19th century.

Xieng Thong means "the golden city." It also means "flame tree." The rear temple wall contains a glass mosaic representation of the *thong* (thong), or tree of life. Mosaic decoration is a relatively recent art form. Colored mosaics depicting local village and court life cover the compounds of two *hor song phra* (hor-son-PHRA), or red side chapels, in Wat Xieng Thong.

Above: **After its construction in the 16th century, Wat Xieng Thong remained under royal patronage until the 1975 revolution swept away the monarchy.**

Opposite: **This carved door at Wat Ong Teu is a good example of Lao design.**

Considered by many to be the most beautiful *wat* in Laos, Wat Xieng Thong embodies all the elegance and refinement of Lao religious architecture. Its breathtakingly dramatic roof is in the Louangphrabang style. Layers overlap one another in a complex and graceful design that swoops so low, they appear to almost touch the ground. Ornate, gold-stenciled designs cover the exterior walls, while the interior contains gold and bronze Buddhas, embroidered tapestries, and finely carved wooden columns.

The complex occupies a superb location overlooking the Mekong. A flight of steps leads directly from the river to the temple compound. In former times this was the main gateway to the city.

98

WOOD CARVING

The Lao have long excelled at wood carving and engraving. Sophisticated craftsmen have been producing decorative religious art for centuries. Large scrolled teak panels on the sides of temples relate scenes from the Ramayana or local myths.

The wooden doors and window shutters of temples are usually decorated with elaborate foliage and figures that fill the surface in crowded but harmonious patterns. These are often painted red and gilded. The gables of temple roofs are made of richly decorated, carved panels in wood and stucco. The roof edges curve upward in order to catch evil spirits.

Many distinctive Buddha statues are made of wood, and fine examples can be seen in the many temples dotting Vientiane and Louangphrabang. An ornate royal funerary chariot at Wat Xieng Thong is made from carved and gilded wood. The chariot's prow is shaped into the form of a five-headed *naga*.

High quality wood carvings and sculptures are also found on the doors, shutters, and gables of recently renovated or reconstructed temples, proving that the art is still very much alive in Laos.

The main sanctuary at Wat Phou is typically Khmer in design.

KHMER RUINS

The combination of high ground and water guaranteed that Phu Pasak, near Champasak in southern Laos, would be a sacred place. The priests of Chenla, the civilization that preceded the Khmer, erected shrines to the mountain gods and water spirits here. A temple already stood at this spot as early as the sixth century.

Wat Phou, the country's great Khmer temple, was built in the 10th century as a shrine to the Hindu deity Shiva. Archaeologists believe that there may have been a road directly connecting Wat Phou with Angkor, 60 miles (97 km) away in Cambodia.

Well-preserved reliefs of Hindu gods and goddesses still decorate the temple's ruined facades. Wat Phou was later converted into a Buddhist temple. The mountain and its sacred spring behind the temple have been the sites of worship and meditation for religious hermits since the 11th century.

Boun Wat Phou, a three-day Buddhist festival, is held at the temple on the full moon of the third lunar month. The festival, which has its origins in the spirit cults of the south, was originally held to appease the guardian *phi* of Wat Phou, and human sacrifices were conducted. Today they have been replaced with a buffalo sacrifice. The festival is one of the largest in Laos. Pilgrims arrive from the south of Laos as well as from neighboring Thai districts. The water tanks at Wat Phou are used for boat racing. Music and dance performances, fireworks, elephant races, and buffalo fights add to the festivities. Buddhism as well as animist rituals incorporating elements of Hinduism are practiced side by side.

A commanding view from the hill above Wat Phou. Some historians believe that nearby Champasak may have been the capital of the Chenla kingdom.

Relating the story of the Phravet, this sumptuous, wooden gilded mural is stretched like a panel at the entrance to Wat Mai.

WAT MAI

Wat Mai, whose name means "the new monastery," is another Lao architectural treasure. The temple, which is topped with a distinctive five-tiered red roof, took more than 70 years to complete. The veranda ceiling, which displays lotus blossoms and scenes from the Buddha's life, is one of the best-preserved murals of its kind in Laos.

Wat Mai's most striking feature is the extraordinary golden bas-relief that runs along the facade. This tells the story of the Phravet, one of the last incarnations of the Buddha. Set in a rural background, it depicts scenes of village life that are clearly Lao. A closer look even reveals small depictions of Louangphrabang landmarks such as That Chomsi and Wat Xieng Thong. The episodes read like a text from left to right. A long beam above the frieze, carved in red and gold relief, highlights settings from the Ramayana.

LAOTIAN LOOMS

Traditionally Lao women expressed themselves creatively by weaving highly complex textiles.

Lao weavers are among the finest in Southeast Asia. Textiles are very important to all Tai societies. In Laos the continued popularity of the women's national dress has helped to sustain an art that has vanished elsewhere.

In traditional Lao society, an ability to weave was a prerequisite for marriage. Even today, especially among the highland ethnic minorities, it is believed that the best way to a man's heart is through a woman's weaving. A woman who is known to be a deft weaver accrues more status than an average weaver.

Looms are often located among the piles that support the house, as this is a cool and shady place to work. Cotton and silk are spun by hand. There is only one cotton harvest a year, but silk can be harvested four times annually. Silk weavers must feed the worms with mulberry leaves to get good yields.

The French introduced chemical dyes to Laos. Since the revolution, there has been a revival in the use of dyes from natural sources. These take longer to obtain. To expert eyes, however, these colors are much richer and more saturated. Red comes from breadfruit and rain trees, indigo from the indigo plant, black from pounded ebony seeds, and yellow from turmeric roots.

Buddhist and animist symbols often appear as traditional motifs in Lao textiles. Other common themes include flowers, hooks, diamonds, *nagas*, casuarina trees, and stylized figures of peacocks, elephants, geese, and dragons. Many old techniques and designs have been lost because of war and population displacement among ethnic groups that were leading exponents of the weaving traditions. It is vital that these old skills be renewed as soon as possible, before they are lost forever.

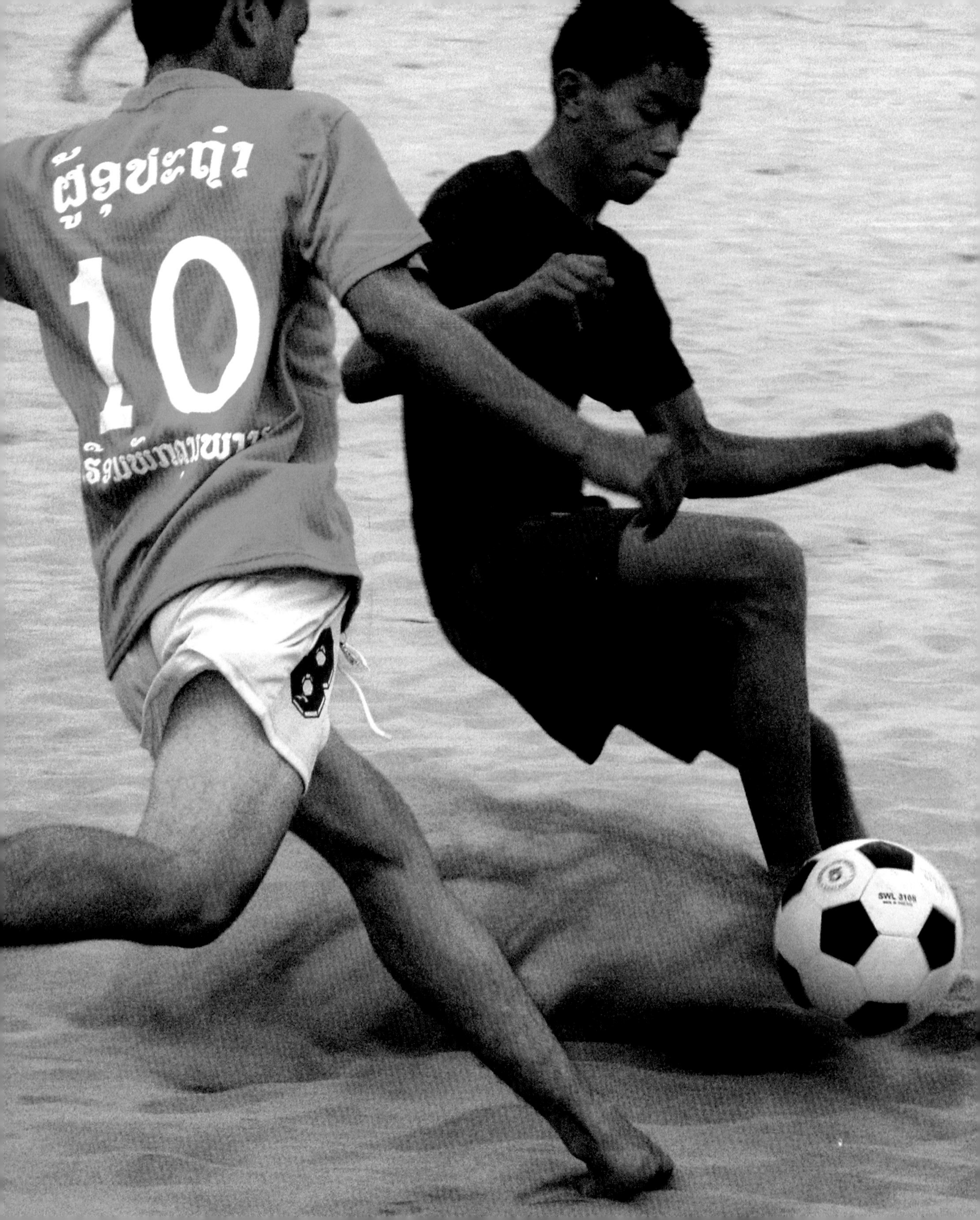
ຜູ້ອຸປະຖໍາ
10

LEISURE

THE PURSUIT OF LEISURE, in the Western sense of the word, is a concept that applies only to the wealthy or more fashion-conscious in Lao cities. Few people are familiar with sports and pastimes such as tennis and golf. Computer and video games are virtually unheard of.

For most Lao, the notion of developing a hobby or setting aside time for planned leisure activities is unusual. The Lao are noted for being a relaxed and easygoing people. They believe that an activity is best avoided if it is not fun, because it will probably cause stress. Lao do not have to be told to slow down and relax. The attitude is inbred.

Above: **A Lao boy readies his homemade kite for flight.**

Opposite: **Soccer is a popular sport among many of the Lao.**

Festivals are important to the Lao, as they provide the chance for family gatherings. Highland ethnic groups often visit Lao cities to participate in festivities or to sell their wares to the lowland Lao. There is rarely spare money for holidays or excursions. Pleasure is derived from the simple, enduring things in life.

Many Lao enjoy tuning into entertainment programs from neighboring countries. They have seven television broadcast stations, including a Vietnamese channel, to choose from. Only 90,000 homes have telephones, and a minuscule 25,000 are wired to the Internet. Years of war and deprivation have obliged the population to maintain a traditional way of life that continues relatively unchanged, especially in rural areas. Leisure activities revolve, as they always have, around the pleasures of family life, the community, and religious practices.

A man strums his guitar while his friends play a form of checkers with bottle caps.

International trends are gradually influencing Lao pop music. The country's first rap/hip-hop band was Overdance.

CITY PASTIMES

Fast-modernizing Vientiane provides city dwellers with a diverse range of leisure activities. Popular pastimes include window shopping in the capital's stores and hanging out at cafés with friends.

Film is a universal pleasure, and going to the movies is a popular pastime with the Lao. The country has no film industry of its own, so most films are dubbed into Lao from Tamil and Mandarin. Thai films are usually shown in their original versions. Very few Lao dine at restaurants, but those who can afford it socialize at bars and beer gardens dotting the banks of rivers. For the people of Vientiane a trip out to one of the cafés, bars, or stalls that have sprung up around the Friendship Bridge has become a popular excursion. Young people are more inclined, though, to spend their time motorbiking around town; listening to mainstream Lao pop, which resembles Thai-style music; or attending one of Vientiane's nightly discos.

SPORTS AND GAMES

Part of the Communist ideology of the post-1975 era was to develop a healthy and vigorous nation through sports. Most Lao cities have a sports stadium. Some were built at the expense of other civil amenities such as good roads. Sports stadiums also serve as venues for concerts, National Day celebrations, and political rallies. In cities such as Vientiane, soccer teams regularly work out in the stadiums. Many Lao are immensely proud of their national team's progress to the second qualifying round of the 2006 World Cup.

Another popular pastime is *takraw* (TAHK-raw), a traditional game played with a hollow cane ball. Two teams compete across a net. The players must keep the ball in the air for as long as possible using only their feet, heels, shoulders, and elbows. A skillful team may be able to keep several balls in the air at the same time. *Takraw* is also widely played in Thailand, Burma, and Malaysia. In former times the game received royal patronage. These days it is undergoing a popular revival.

Lao-style boxing is a form of martial art called Muay Lao (MAE-Lao). The carved pillars and stone slabs of ancient Lao temples often depict a variety of poses and steps that are part of the training. The troops of Fa Ngum, the king who first unified the country, are said to have found the discipline useful in battle. Both feet and fists are used in this sport, which resembles a fusion of boxing and karate.

Boys practicing *takraw*, a game popular with many Southeast Asians.

Lao boxing, or Muay Lao, was banned under the French but is now enjoying a revival thanks to the efforts of the government-sponsored Lao Sports Association.

107

Before the revolution, Lao orchestras were far larger and more formal. Many of these were disbanded due to their associations with the royal family. These days, with greater tolerance and freedom of movement, many are re-forming.

A FEAST OF DANCE AND MUSIC

The Lao have music in their blood. Lao musicians depend largely on their memories and improvisational skills. There are very few formal, written compositions. Vocal music is especially popular in Laos, and songs have been passed down from generation to generation. Early traveling minstrels were influenced by the folklore of India. Songs that have survived the passing time often champion love and heroic adventures or espouse prophesies and prayer.

A typical example of Lao melodies is found in their folk music. It uses a popular instrument, the *khene* (ken), which is a kind of harmonica or hand organ made with varying lengths of bamboo tubes. Another common wind instrument is the *khuy* (KOO), a type of bamboo flute. Various percussion instruments and two-string violins are also important. The *khong vong* (ker-ONG VON) is a horseshoe-shaped instrument consisting of 16 small bronze gongs that are struck with wooden mallets. Another common instrument is the *nang nat* (ner-ANG nat), a small xylophone.

HERBAL SAUNAS

The residents of Vientiane have long been able to enjoy healthy relaxation in the form of traditional saunas. These are found in some of the city's temples. The best-known temple for this kind of treatment is Wat Sok Pa Luang, a retreat on the outskirts of Vientiane. The saunas are prepared by Buddhist nuns.

Herbs are mixed with dried eucalyptus and other leaves and burned underneath an elevated wooden sauna room in which four or five people can sit. The pleasant fragrance of burning sap and herbs can be inhaled. The saunas are usually conducted in the early evening. Herbal teas are served on an airy balcony between sessions in the sauna.

The Lao say that for maximum effect, it is best to allow the herbs to soak into the pores of the skin for at least two hours before one takes a bath.

These two instruments are almost always included in *seb noi* (zeb NO-ee) orchestras, which are used in religious processions or at the end of vocal recitals.

Many of the ethnic minorities also have strong musical traditions. A number of the ethnic Khamu, for example, have their own orchestras with clarinets, flutes, xylophones, and single-string violins. For the Khamu, gongs are by far the most important instrument. When someone is ill, deafening music is played to drive out or influence evil spirits.

Where there is music, there is also dance. Classical Lao dance has its origins in India. Styles were probably imported from the Cambodian royal court in the 14th century. There are also Burmese and Thai influences in Lao dance. Scenes from the Ramayana are sometimes performed in temple compounds. There is usually little or no stage scenery, but the sumptuous costumes and colorful lacquered masks more than make up for the absence of elaborate sets.

Young urban Lao seem to prefer to dance to the sounds of Western and Thai pop music in the capital's discos. Somehow a touch of the tradition prevails here as well. No evening is quite complete without at least one *lamvong* (lam-VON), which is a traditional Lao folk dance where two circles are formed, with women on the outside and the men dancing in the inner ring. The *lamvong* is also performed at festivals, weddings, and parties.

For young men of some Lao minorities such as the Hmong, the tradition of serenading girls they wish to marry in the form of a musical dialogue remains an important custom. To the accompaniment of a khene *or another instrument the boy will try to woo the girl with words of flattery as to why he has chosen her. The girl will question him in return, and a dialogue will gradually develop.*

FESTIVALS

THE LAO ARE A FESTIVE PEOPLE, a fact attested to by the number and wealth of national and local festivals held throughout the year. *Boun* (boon) means "festival" in Lao. *Het boun* (HET-boon) signifies "merit making," so *boun*, to the Lao way of thinking, is an opportunity for self-improvement through religious observance and the pursuit of earthly pleasures.

The Lao are happy to celebrate not only their own festivals but those of other groups and cultures as well. New Year's Day is celebrated four times a year: the international New Year in January; the Chinese and Vietnamese New Year (also known as Tet) in January/February; the Lao Buddhist New Year, which falls in April; and finally the Hmong New Year in December.

Left: **Devotees carrying out prayer rituals during the That Luang Festival.**

Opposite: **Young Lao women in their traditional outfits carrying offerings during the Lao New Year.**

THE LAO CALENDAR

The Western Gregorian calendar is used in Laos for all government and business matters. Many people, however, especially in rural areas, still refer to the traditional lunar calendar. The Lao Buddhist calendar is based on the movements of the sun and the moon. Each year is reckoned to begin in December, but the Lao choose to celebrate the beginning of the year in April, which is considered a more auspicious month. The Lao calendar is a combination of the old Khmer and Sino-Vietnamese ones, in which each year is named after a different animal. During the Lao New Year celebrations, paper pennants bearing images of the animal for that year are sold. Because the Lao Buddhist year follows a lunar calendar, the timing of many festivals varies from year to year.

Trance sword dancers draw an audience during a Lao festival.

MAJOR FESTIVALS

While there are many small annual *boun* centered on local pagodas, there are also several major regional celebrations, such as the Wat Phou Festival in Champasak in the south. The four most important festivals in Laos are the Lao New Year (Pi Mai), the Rocket Festival (Boun Bang Fay), the Water Festival (Boun Lay Heua Fay), and the That Luang Festival (Boun That Luang). The following list also includes other main religious and secular events on the Lao calendar.

JANUARY: Boun Phra Vet Held to celebrate King Vessantara's reincarnation as a Buddha.

JANUARY/FEBRUARY: Chinese and Vietnamese New Year (Tet) A time for dances, processions, and fireworks.

APRIL: Lao New Year (Pi Mai) The preferred date for the Lao New Year.

MAY: Visakha Puja A festival celebrating the birth, enlightenment, and death of the Buddha.

In May, Labor Day, an event honoring workers the world over, is celebrated in Vientiane with colorful parades.

Ladies dressed in their traditional costumes bring offerings of rice, money and flowers to the monks of That Luang Temple in Vientiane.

In October, Awk Phansa celebrates the end of the Buddhist Lent. Parties are held, and boat races take place on the Mekong River.

MAY: The Rocket Festival (Boun Bang Fay) A Buddhist rain-making festival.

JULY: Khao Phansa The beginning of Buddhist Lent. A time for religious retreats and fasting.

AUGUST/ SEPTEMBER: Haw Khao Padap Din A festival during which the living pay their respects to the dead. Many cremations are held at this time.

NOVEMBER: That Luang Festival A colorful event focusing on the country's most important temple.

DECEMBER: Lao National Day A national holiday to celebrate the 1975 revolution.

PI MAI

Few festivals evoke the life and customs of the people better than the Lao New Year, or Pi Mai. Pi Mai is known in Laos as the Fifth Month Festival.

Lao astrologers decided to delay the official year by several months so that the New Year would start under more favorable conditions. The astrological signs at this particular time are believed to point to light and prosperity. The period also anticipates the end of the hot season and the advent of the life-sustaining rains.

Before the festival begins, each house is meticulously cleaned and swept to banish evil spirits. Temples and homes also receive a fresh coat of paint.

The festival is an occasion for the Lao to dress up in their best and visit temples. The Lao pray for a good crop and pay homage to the city's most important Buddha statues. It is the monks' task to ritually cleanse

A beauty queen passes the former royal palace in Louangphrabang during a Pi Mai procession. Louangphrabang is generally acknowledged to be the best place to see the festival. Many of the event's original elements, long since discarded in other regions, remain unchanged here.

A line of women make their way along Louangphrabang's main street—the best place to view the Pi Mai procession.

Buddha images with perfumed holy water filled with flowers. Water is a strong symbol of purification. Often monks and passersby on the streets are doused with pails of water.

Votive mounds in the shape of miniature stupas are constructed with sand in the compounds of temples or along the banks of the Mekong River. Pi Mai is a serious occasion but not a solemn one. During the day and evening Vientiane is alive with parades, beauty contests, musical and dance recitals, dramas, and fairs.

Deep in their heart, the Lao remain staunchly conservative and traditional people. During Pi Mai, young Lao visit their families, elders, and superiors to pay their respect. Kneeling humbly before their elders, they pour fragrant water over their hands and seek blessings and good fortune for the coming year.

BACI *CEREMONY*

The *baci* ceremony is unique to Tai races and central to Lao culture. The animist ritual is believed to predate Buddhism. *Baci* are held to celebrate special events and occasions such as marriages, births, visits from guests, and homecomings.

They are also held during festivals and private parties. In Laos novice monks are given a *baci* before they enter the *wat*, mothers are honored

Conducting a *baci*, the most important of all Lao spiritual ceremonies.

Lao festivals have much in common with those in other Southeast Asian countries, particularly Thailand. What makes Lao festivals unique is their retention of many original elements that have been lost or rejected elsewhere. Less commercialized than neighboring countries' cultural events and more elemental and closer to their animist roots, Lao festivals represent the closest link to many of the pre-Buddhist rites and practices that once thrived throughout the region.

with one after they have recovered from giving birth, and visiting officials often receive a *baci*. *Baci* are usually conducted by a respected elder, sometimes in the presence of a monk.

Besides generating goodwill and hospitality, the *baci* aims to restore balance and harmony to the individual and the community. The ceremony is also dedicated to the sick in the hope of providing a cure. The Lao believe that the body is protected by 32 spirits called *kwan* (KWA-ang). For a person to enjoy perfect health and balance, all 32 *kwan* must be present. The departure of even one will bring about illness and even possible death. As guests pray on, the person conducting the ritual chants in a mix of Lao and Pali, invoking both Buddhist and animist deities and spirits, all the while calling for the *kwan* to return.

Central to the ceremony is an arrangement of flowers, white cotton strings, banana leaves, and candles called a *phakwan* (PA-kwang). White threads are taken from the *phakwan* and tied around the guests' wrists with blessings and good wishes. The threads should not be removed for at least three days. A meal is served after the ceremony. This is often followed by the *lamvong*, the national dance.

Anyone lucky enough to attend a *baci* will recognize the warmth and sincerity of this ancient ceremony as well as realize its importance as a social and family bond. For the Lao, the *baci* is a unique way of confirming the value of life.

WHITE EQUALS HARMONY

In Laos, the color white is a symbol of peace, harmony, good fortune, and human warmth and community. The cotton threads used in the *baci* ceremony are always white.

THE ROCKET FESTIVAL

Like the *baci* ceremony, Boun Bang Fay, or the Rocket Festival, is a good example of the Lao propensity to mix Buddhism and animism. *Bang* (BA-an) means "bamboo pipe," and *fay* (fey) is "fire." The festival is traditionally held on the day of the full moon during the sixth month of the lunar calendar.

The official purpose of the festival is to commemorate the life and achievements of the Buddha. Pilgrimages and merit making are important parts of the events. A more earthy side to the festival, harking back to ancient fertility rites, is associated with the rockets themselves. These are fired into the sky in the symbolic hope of releasing the rains.

The rockets, which are covered in tinfoil and colorful streamers, are made of bamboo and may be as long as 6 feet (1.8 m). The rockets are carried through the streets to the accompaniment of drums, *khene*, and songs. The rocket that soars the highest will bring the most prestige to its makers. In former times the rockets were made exclusively by the temple authorities. Today they are made by villages, government departments, schools, and trade union groups as well.

A celebrant at the Rocket Festival.

For visitors, the festival is a good chance to enjoy Lao music and dance, as well as performances of *maw lum* (moor LOOM), a traditional folk musical that is both bawdy and comical. For rural Lao, Boun Bang Fay is the last chance for high spirits before the hard work in the rice fields begins in earnest.

119

FOOD

LAO FOOD IS OFTEN compared with Thai cuisine, but the Chinese influence is more subtle. Glutinous rice is the main staple, and dishes are liberally doused with spices such as ginger, tamarind, lemongrass, and several types of hot chili peppers. A typical Lao dish is a mixture of fiery and fragrant flavors, moderated by herbs. Because the country has no access to the sea, fish come fresh from the Mekong and other rivers.

Identifying Lao cooking is easy. If it mixes fish, meat, and herbs in the same dish, it is the real McCoy. *Pa dek* (pah DEK), or fermented fish, and *nam pa* (nahm PAH), or fish sauce, are vital staples—though their distinctive smell takes some getting used to. Food is usually prepared on a stove fired by wood or charcoal.

Left: **An elegant Lao meal served in a Louangphrabang restaurant.**

Opposite: **A food vendor prepares a typical Lao dish of grilled chicken.**

The kitchen garden commands an important place in Lao homes. Vegetables such as onions, yams, cucumbers, salad greens, eggplants, beans, spinach, and shallots are grown there. Condiments such as citronella, hot peppers, and ginger may also be cultivated. Each house normally has its own fruit trees as well. Residents simply reach out and pluck bananas, coconuts, mangoes, avocados, lychees, guavas, and durians from their gardens when the fruit are in season. These home products supplement food that is bought in the open market. All these are essential ingredients in many Lao religious practices. Anyone who has attended a *baci* ceremony or witnessed monks on their morning alms rounds would be familiar with this fact.

Right: **A selection of green vegetables and condiments at a Lao market.**

Opposite: **Glutinous rice is a staple in Lao cuisine.**

BASKETS OF RICE

Rice is highly esteemed in Laos. The Lao are especially partial to sticky or glutinous rice, *khao nyao* (kah-OH nya-o). Family members may eat from a communal bowl or have their own individual baskets. Sticky rice is eaten with the fingers. Rice is rolled into a tight ball and then used as an eating utensil to push and scoop up other ingredients on the plate or is dipped into sauces.

The sweet-toothed Lao also add rice to various desserts and sweets. The versatile grain can be mixed with taro, coconut milk, or water-lily roots. *Khao tom* (kah-OH tom) consists of rice combined with coconut milk and bananas and then steamed in a banana leaf. Another popular dessert, *tom nam hua bua* (tom nahm WHOO-er boo-er), is prepared by mixing coconut milk and lotus flowers.

Rice remains a powerful, life-affirming symbol throughout Asia. In Laos sticky rice is often pressed onto Buddha statues and the walls of private homes as offerings to the resident spirit. Women are strongly associated with rice. In many remote villages, a legend holds that the rice goddess sacrificed her body in a fire, and the ashes helped to produce a bumper crop for the village. In some Phuan villages, the bones of female ancestors are preserved in a stupa in the middle of the family's rice fields.

Some of the typical condiments used in Lao cooking.

POPULAR DISHES

In addition to freshwater fish, the Lao get their protein from pork, chicken, water buffalo, and duck. Deer, quail, wild chickens, and small birds are also eaten. The traditional ceremonial dish of the Lao and the closest thing to a national dish is called *laap* (laap). The word means "luck." *Laap* is an indispensable dish for special occasions and for honored guests. Often compared with steak tartar or Mexican seviche, meat-based *laap* is made by mixing finely minced beef, chicken, pork, and venison. However, if these are not available, then water buffalo with chopped mint and lemon juice is used. There is also a fish-based version of *laap*.

Those on a budget may wish to sample inexpensive Lao cuisine in markets or at street stalls. One favorite choice is *tam maak hung* (taam MAK hoong), a spicy green papaya salad. This is made by pounding green papaya, lime juice, chilies, garlic, *padek* (fermented fish sauce) and whatever else comes to hand in a big mortar.

Thai-style curries are popular as well. These dishes are spiced with numbingly hot red chilies but cooled down with the use of slightly sweet coconut milk. The Lao also enjoy Vietnamese food. The most common dish is *foe* (fow) or *pho*—a rice-noodle soup. *Foe* is usually served with a side plate of salad vegetables such as lettuce, mint, and bean sprouts, which can be added to the broth. *Foe* is a popular snack and breakfast dish. Soup accompanies most main meals and is always served in the middle or toward the end, never at the beginning.

FRENCH LEGACIES

Many of the old French buildings in Laos may be crumbling, but the French food legacy is as strong as ever. French cuisine is widely available in Vientiane and Louangphrabang. Frog legs and filet mignon, a steak dish, remain popular with Lao who can afford such luxuries. French-style baguettes are common breakfast items. These are sold fresh at the morning markets and bakeries. The bread is dipped into hot milky coffee and eaten with fried eggs or condensed milk. Alternatively one can tuck into baguettes the Lao way: sprinkle fish sauce on top or make a sandwich with a pâté filling.

French croissants and *pains au chocolat* (pan o SHO-co-la), or rolls filled with chocolate, are eaten in street cafés with cups of strong Lao coffee. Visitors to Vientiane are often surprised to find bottles of old wines such as Bordeaux and Bergerac being proudly carried from the cellars of French restaurants.

French bread is a popular item in the morning. The Lao often buy their breakfast baguettes stuffed with Lao-style pâté.

MANNERS AT THE LAO TABLE

Lao family meals seem like relaxed and informal events, but there are certain customs and manners to be observed. Unlike in Western countries, where people sit around a raised table, the Lao are more likely to squat on the floor around one or more circular bamboo tables. Instead of a succession of courses served one after the other, food is laid out on the table in several dishes at the beginning of the meal. The family and any guests help themselves, eating whatever they like in no particular order.

There are certain attitudes connected to food and its consumption that foreigners may not be aware of. One of these is the Lao concept of *piep* (pyee-EP). It can be roughly translated as "status," "dignity," or "sense

Eating with one's hand is a custom common not just in Laos but also in many other Asian countries.

of prestige." At Lao family meals, this means that elders and the most senior-ranking members of the family always take the first mouthful. Other members follow according to age. From this point onward everyone is free to eat whatever they fancy, but no one should help himself before an older family member has first tried a dish. It is also inadvisable to reach for food at the same time as someone else. Guests should not continue eating after everyone else has finished. It is the custom in Laos to always leave something on the plate when one has finished the meal. If a guest does not do this, the host will lose *piep*, as it is understood that he did not provide enough food, leaving the guest hungry.

The Lao are meticulously clean and have the habit of washing their hands not only before but also after a meal.

An eye-catching array of river fish from the Mekong.

DRINKS

The Lao enjoy natural drinks such as coconut milk and their own local brew *lau-lao* (LA-oo-lao), which is a fermented rice wine. Coconut milk is often mixed with other fruit juices, while white *lau-lao* is sometimes drunk with a twist of lime or even with cola. *Fanthong* (fahn-TONG) is a red *lau-lao* fermented with herbs. It is the custom at parties, festivals, and other social gatherings for several people to drink *lau-lao* from clay jugs using long straws. *Beer Lao* is a light lager with 5 percent alcohol content. It is consumed ice cold.

Cinnamon sticks are used in cooking to lend extra flavor.

Lao coffee is excellent. Most of it comes from the fertile Bolovens Plateau in southern Laos. Roasted and ground, it is filtered with hot water in a socklike bag before being served in cafés and restaurants. The Lao prefer their coffee thick and sweet, so sugar and condensed milk are freely added. You can also enjoy it cold by adding crushed ice. Traditionally coffee is served with a complimentary glass of *naam sa* (nam SAH), or weak Chinese tea. Both black Indian tea and cured or green Chinese tea are common in Laos.

Laos produces a small quantity of black tea but not enough to be self-sufficient.

LAU-LAO: THE RICE SPIRIT

Lau-lao is sold in bottles. As it is locally brewed, the taste may vary from town to town. Even the government distils its own brand, called Sticky Rice.

Most distillers sell *lau-lao* in whatever container they happen to have around, so it is advisable to check if the bottle of soft drink in hand is really what it appears to be. Otherwise you may be unpleasantly surprised by the innocent-looking clear liquid!

During festivities and gatherings the host kicks off proceedings by pouring a shot of *lau-lao* and tossing it to the ground or a wall to pay respect to and appease the local spirit. The host then pours himself a shot and gulps it down. Any remaining drops are emptied on the floor before the glass is passed to the next person and filled. The host will serve each guest in turn.

Once the round is completed, the host presents the *lau-lao* and the glass to the first guest. This guest then serves himself before pouring for the other guests, one at a time. When everyone present has had a share of the alcohol, the *lau-lao* and the glass are passed on to the second guest, and the cycle is repeated. Everyone is expected to drink at least one shot so that the house spirit and the host are not offended.

TOM SOM (SHREDDED GREEN PAPAYA SALAD)

¼ pound (125 g) string beans, cut into 1-inch (2.5 cm) lengths
2 cloves garlic
3 small green chilies (add fewer if a less spicy version is preferred)
1 small papaya (1 pound, 500 g), halved, peeled, and seeded
1 carrot, peeled
1 medium tomato, cut into thin wedges
2 tablespoons fresh lime juice
1 tablespoon fish sauce (available in Asian stores)
1 tablespoon sugar
1 cup fresh cilantro leaves (optional)
½ cup (75 g) chopped unsalted roasted peanuts

Fill a saucepan three-quarters full of water and bring to a boil. Add string beans and blanch for one minute. Drain, then set beans aside. Pound the garlic and chilies in a mortar to form a coarse paste. Add the beans, pound the mixture quickly, and transfer contents to a salad bowl. Use a grater to shred the papaya and carrot into long, thin slivers. Pound the papaya and carrot slivers in small batches to bruise them. Transfer to the bean mixture, and add tomato wedges. Stir the lime juice, fish sauce, and sugar in a small bowl until the sugar dissolves completely. Pour liquid over the vegetables and mix thoroughly. Garnish with cilantro and peanuts.

SANGKHANYA MAK UEH (COCONUT CUSTARD STEAMED IN PUMPKIN)

1 medium pumpkin, 8 inches (20 cm) wide
10 eggs
1 cup (200 g) sugar
8 ½ ounces (250 ml) coconut milk
Pinch of salt

Cut off the top of the pumpkin and remove the seeds. Retain the pumpkin top as a lid. Beat the eggs with sugar, coconut milk, and salt. Pour the mixture into the pumpkin, cover with the pumpkin lid, and steam on a stovetop for one hour. Wait for it to cool, then cut the pumpkin into wedges and serve.

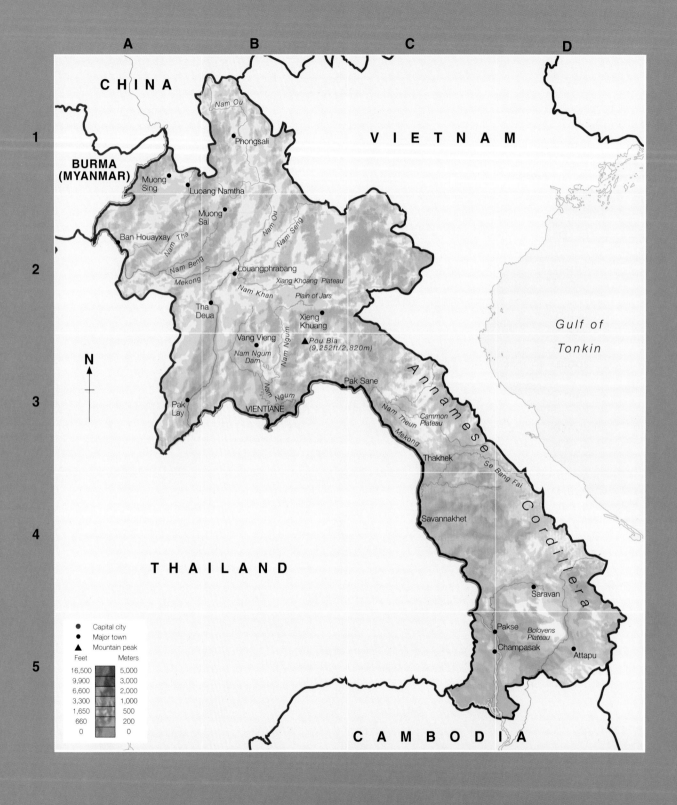

MAP OF LAOS

ECONOMIC LAOS

Services

✈ Airport

🚢 Seaports

🧳 Tourism

Natural Resources

💎 Gemstones (Sapphires)

🐟 Fish

🪵 Timber

🪵 Rubber

🟫 Gold

Cu Copper

⚙ Hydropower

Agriculture

🌾 Rice

☕ Tea

● Coffee

🌿 Sugarcane

🥬 Vegetables

🍂 Potash

🫘 Cardamom

👕 Cotton

Industry

🎋 Textiles

▨ Weaving

🥤 Food and beverage processing

🍺 Beer

▢ Paper processing

ABOUT
THE ECONOMY

OVERVIEW

The Communist state embarked on decentralization and encouraged private enterprise in 1986. This resulted in growth, but Laos lacks basic infrastructure. Subsistence agriculture, dominated by rice cultivation, employs 80 percent of the country's workforce and contributes half of the gross domestic product. An international aid recipient, Laos is considering becoming a member of the World Trade Organization in the coming years.

GROSS DOMESTIC PRODUCT (GDP)

$12.61 billion (2007 estimate)

GDP GROWTH

7 percent (2007 estimate)

INFLATION RATE

5 percent (2007 estimate)

EXTERNAL DEBT

$3.2 billion (2006 estimate)

CURRENCY

Kip (LAK)
US$1 = 9,658 LAK (2007)
The kip is available only in paper notes. Laos has no coins.

NATURAL RESOURCES

Timber, hydropower, gold, tin, copper, gemstones

AGRICULTURAL PRODUCTS

Rice, cardamom, coffee, cotton, corn, soybeans, sugarcane, sweet potatoes, tobacco, vegetables, poultry

INDUSTRY

Agricultural processing, construction, electric power, garments, mining, tourism

MAJOR EXPORTS

Coffee, electricity, garments, tin, wood products

MAJOR IMPORTS

Consumer goods, fuel, machinery and equipment, vehicles

MAIN TRADE PARTNERS

Thailand, Vietnam, China (2006 estimate)

WORKFORCE

2.1 million—80 percent in agriculture, 20 percent in industry and services (2006 estimate)

UNEMPLOYMENT RATE

2.4 percent (2005 estimate)

POPULATION BELOW POVERTY LINE

30.7 percent (2005 estimate)

ECONOMIC AID

$379 million (2006 estimate)

CULTURAL LAOS

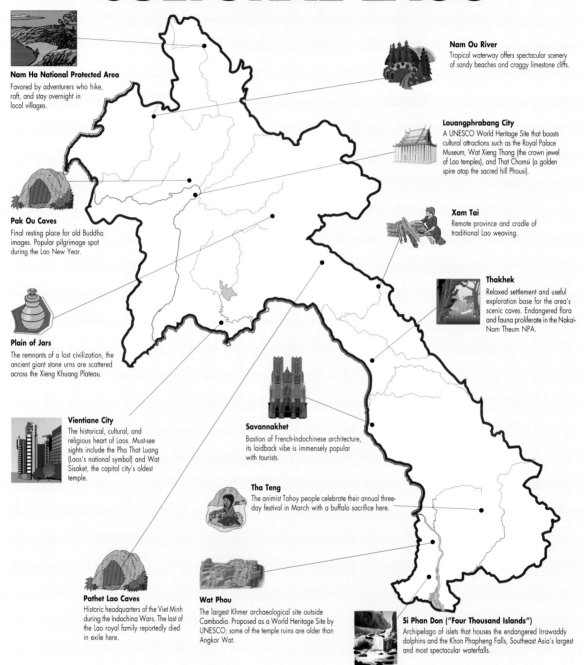

Nam Ha National Protected Area
Favored by adventurers who hike, raft, and stay overnight in local villages.

Nam Ou River
Tropical waterway offers spectacular scenery of sandy beaches and craggy limestone cliffs.

Louangphrabang City
A UNESCO World Heritage Site that boasts cultural attractions such as the Royal Palace Museum, Wat Xieng Thong (the crown jewel of Lao temples), and That Chomsi (a golden spire atop the sacred hill Phousi).

Pak Ou Caves
Final resting place for old Buddha images. Popular pilgrimage spot during the Lao New Year.

Xam Tai
Remote province and cradle of traditional Lao weaving.

Thakhek
Relaxed settlement and useful exploration base for the area's scenic caves. Endangered flora and fauna proliferate in the Nakai-Nam Theum NPA.

Plain of Jars
The remnants of a lost civilization, the ancient giant stone urns are scattered across the Xieng Khuang Plateau.

Vientiane City
The historical, cultural, and religious heart of Laos. Must-see sights include the Pha That Luang (Laos's national symbol) and Wat Sisaket, the capital city's oldest temple.

Savannakhet
Bastion of French-Indochinese architecture, its laidback vibe is immensely popular with tourists.

Tha Teng
The animist Tahoy people celebrate their annual three-day festival in March with a buffalo sacrifice here.

Pathet Lao Caves
Historic headquarters of the Viet Minh during the Indochina Wars. The last of the Lao royal family reportedly died in exile here.

Wat Phou
The largest Khmer archaeological site outside Cambodia. Proposed as a World Heritage Site by UNESCO; some of the temple ruins are older than Angkor Wat.

Si Phan Don ("Four Thousand Islands")
Archipelago of islets that houses the endangered Irrawaddy dolphins and the Khon Phapheng Falls, Southeast Asia's largest and most spectacular waterfalls.

ABOUT THE CULTURE

OFFICIAL NAME
Lao People's Democratic Republic (LPDR)

FLAG DESCRIPTION
Three horizontal bands—red stripes at the top and the bottom, with a central blue band that is twice as wide. A white circle sits in the center of the blue band. The red symbolizes blood shed during the country's long civil war, and the blue represents the Mekong River. The white circle symbolizes the people's unity.

INDEPENDENCE
July 19, 1949

CAPITAL
Vientiane (Vieng Chan)

MAJOR CITIES
Vientiane, Louangphrabang, Pakse, Savannakhet

POPULATION
6.5 million (2007 estimate)

BIRTHRATE
35 births per 1,000 Lao (2007 estimate)

DEATH RATE
11.3 deaths per 1,000 Lao (2007 estimate)

LIFE EXPECTANCY
55.9 years (2007 estimate)

ETHNIC GROUPS
Lao Lum, 68 percent; Lao Theung, 22 percent; Lao Soung (including the Hmong and the Yao), 9 percent; ethnic Chinese/Vietnamese, 1 percent (2007 estimate)

RELIGIOUS GROUPS
Buddhist, 65 percent; animist, 33 percent; Christian, 1.3 percent; others, 0.7 percent

MAIN LANGUAGES
Lao (official), French, English, various indigenous languages and dialects

LITERACY RATE
68.7 percent (2007 estimate)

IMPORTANT HOLIDAYS
New Year (January 1), Pathet Lao Day (January 6), Chinese and Vietnamese New Year (January/ February), Women's Day (March 8), Lao People's Party Day (March 22), Lao New Year (April), Labor Day (May 1), Rocket Festival (May), Children's Day (June 1), Lao Issara (August 13), Liberation Day (August 23), Freedom from France Day (October 12), That Luang Festival (November), National Day (December 2)

TIME LINE

IN LAOS	IN THE WORLD
10,000 B.C.	
Descended from hunter-gatherers, the early people of Laos settle along the Mekong River.	
	323 B.C.
A.D.100	Alexander the Great's empire stretches from Greece to India.
Indian settlers establish foundation of Theravada Buddhism.	
900	
The Khmer come into power and establish Angkor as their capital.	**1206–1368**
1353	Genghis Khan unifies the Mongols and starts conquest of the world. At its height, the Mongol Empire under Kublai Khan stretches from China to Persia and parts of Europe and Russia.
Fa Ngum conquers Louangphrabang and establishes Lane Xang.	
1479	
Vietnam invades Lane Xang.	**1558–1603**
1563	Reign of Elizabeth I of England
King Setthathirat moves the capital of Lane Xang from Louangphrabang to Vieng Chan (Vientiane).	
1571	
Setthathirat dies. Burma invades and occupies Lane Xang.	
1637–94	
Lane Xang's golden age: King Souligna Vongsa reestablishes kingdom as an independent state.	
1700s–1800s	
Period of instability. Lane Xang separates into three kingdoms, which are repeatedly invaded.	**1776**
	U.S. Declaration of Independence
1826	**1789–99**
Lao king Chao Anou is killed after a failed rebellion against Siam. Vientiane is razed.	The French Revolution

IN LAOS	IN THE WORLD
1893 France colonizes Laos.	
1939 Japanese forces control Laos.	**1939** World War II begins.
1945–46 World War II ends. Start of First Indochina War.	**1945** The United States drops atomic bombs on Hiroshima and Nagasaki.
1949–50 Laos gains independence from France.	**1949** The North Atlantic Treaty Organization (NATO) is formed.
1954 Vietnam defeats France, leading to Communist takeover in Indochina.	
1960 Start of Second Indochina War.	
1975 Pathet Lao establishes the Lao People's Democratic Republic (LPDR), a Communist state. Kaysone Phomvihan is appointed president.	
1986 Decentralization and introduction of a market economy.	**1986** Nuclear power disaster at Chernobyl in Ukraine
1992 Laos establishes relations with United States. Khamtay Siphandone is appointed president.	
1994 Friendship Bridge links Laos with Thailand.	
1997 Laos joins the Association of Southeast Asian Nations (ASEAN).	**1997** Hong Kong is returned to China.
2006 Former minister of defense Choummali Saignason becomes president of Laos.	**2003** War in Iraq begins.

GLOSSARY

baci (BAH-see, su khwan)
Ritual held to celebrate special occasions such as marriages, births, and homecomings.

boun (boon)
Festival.

het boun (HET-boon)
Merit making.

jataka (jah-TAK-er)
Incarnations of the Buddha.

kampi (kem-PI)
Lao manuscripts, usually engraved on palm leaves and threaded together with cord.

kha dong (kaa DONG)
Dowry or bride price paid by the groom.

khene (ken)
Hand organ or harmonica made from varying lengths of bamboo tubes.

khong vong (ker-ONG VON)
Horseshoe-shaped musical instrument made up of 16 small bronze gongs that are struck with wooden mallets.

khuy (KOO)
A type of bamboo flute.

kwan (KWA-ang)
Spirits that protect the body.

laap (laap)
A traditional ceremonial dish, served on special occasions or to honored guests. It is made from finely minced beef and venison, with chopped mint and lemon juice.

lau-lao (LA-oo-lao)
Fermented rice wine.

mudra
Attitude, or the way the Buddha images are represented.

naga (NAR-ger)
Mythical water serpent that resembles a cobra. In Lao it is refered to as nak.

nang nat (ner-ANG nat)
Small xylophone.

paa beuk (PAH buk)
Giant Mekong catfish, the world's largest freshwater fish.

phakwan (PA-kwang)
An arrangement of flowers, white cotton strings, banana leaves, and candles for a baci.

phi (PEE)
Guardian spirit.

takraw (TAHK-raw)
Traditional game played with a hollow cane ball.

wat (what)
Pagoda or temple.

FURTHER INFORMATION

BOOKS

Dramer, Kim. *Mekong River.* New York: Franklin Watts, 2001

Fay, Kim. *To Asia with Love.* Singapore: Things Asian Press, 2004

O'Tailan, Jack. *Footprint: Laos.* Bath, England: Footprint, 2006

Tapp, Nicholas and Yee, Gary Yia. *The Hmong/ Miao in Asia.* Chiang Mai, Thailand: Silkworm Books, 2004

Warner, Roger. *Shooting at the Moon: The Story of America's Clandestine War in Laos.* Hanover, Germany: Steerforth Press, 2006

WEBSITES

Ecotourism Laos. www.ecotourismlaos.com

Muong Lao. www.muonglao.com

Nam Ha Protected Area. www.theboatlanding.laopdr.com/npa.html

Trade Environment Database (TED) Case Studies: Laos and Hydroelectric Power. www.american.edu/projects/mandala/TED/laosdam.htm

Visit Laos. www.visit-laos.com

FILMS

Air America. Carolco Pictures, 1990

BIBLIOGRAPHY

Asian Development Bank. *ADB Country Strategy and Program: Lao People's Democratic Republic 2007–2011*. Manila: Asian Development Bank, 2006.

Burke, Andrew and Justine Vaisutis. *Lonely Planet: Laos*. Victoria, Australia: Lonely Planet Publications, 2007.

Cheeseman, Patricia. *Costume and Culture*. Thailand: Studio Naenna Co., 1990.

Hamilton, Wanda. *Favorite Stories from Laos* and *More Favorite Stories from Laos*. Singapore: Heinemann Asia, 1990.

Hoskins, John and Allen W. Hopkins. *The Mekong: A River and Its People*. Bangkok: Post Publishing Co., 1991.

Jue, June. *Savoring Southeast Asia*. Singapore: Five Mile Press, 2000.

Kaignavongsa, Xay and Hugh Fincher. *Legends of the Lao*. Bangkok: Geodata Systems, 1993.

Mahoney, Therese Mary. *The White Parasol and the Red Star: The Lao Classical Music Culture in a Climate of Change*. Ann Arbor, MI: University of Michigan Press, 2001.

Pholsena, Watthana. *Postwar Laos: The Politics of Culture, History, and Identity*. Singapore: Institute of Southeast Asian Studies, 2006.

Schuettler, Darren. "Laos Defends Dam Project Against Environmental Critics." Bangkok: Reuters News Service, September 1, 2004.

Tan, Su-Lyn. *Foodlore and Flavors: Inside the Southeast Asian Kitchen*. Kuala Lumpur: ArtPost Asia, 2007.

Zickgraf, Ralph. *Places and Peoples'of the World: Laos*. New York: Chelsea House, 1990.

Asia Food Recipes. http://asiarecipe.com/Laos.html

Central Intelligence Agency World Factbook (select Laos from country list). www.cia.gov/cia/publications/factbook/index.html

Lao National Committee for Energy. www.poweringprogress.org/nt2/background.htm

Mongabay: Laos–The Economy. www.mongabay.com/reference/country_studies/laos/ECONOMY.html

MSN Encarta–Laos. http://Encarta.msn.com/encyclopedia_761551958/laos.html

UNESCO. www.unescobkk.org/index.php?id=4364

INDEX